INSIDE THE WORLDS OF
STAR WARS
TRILOGY

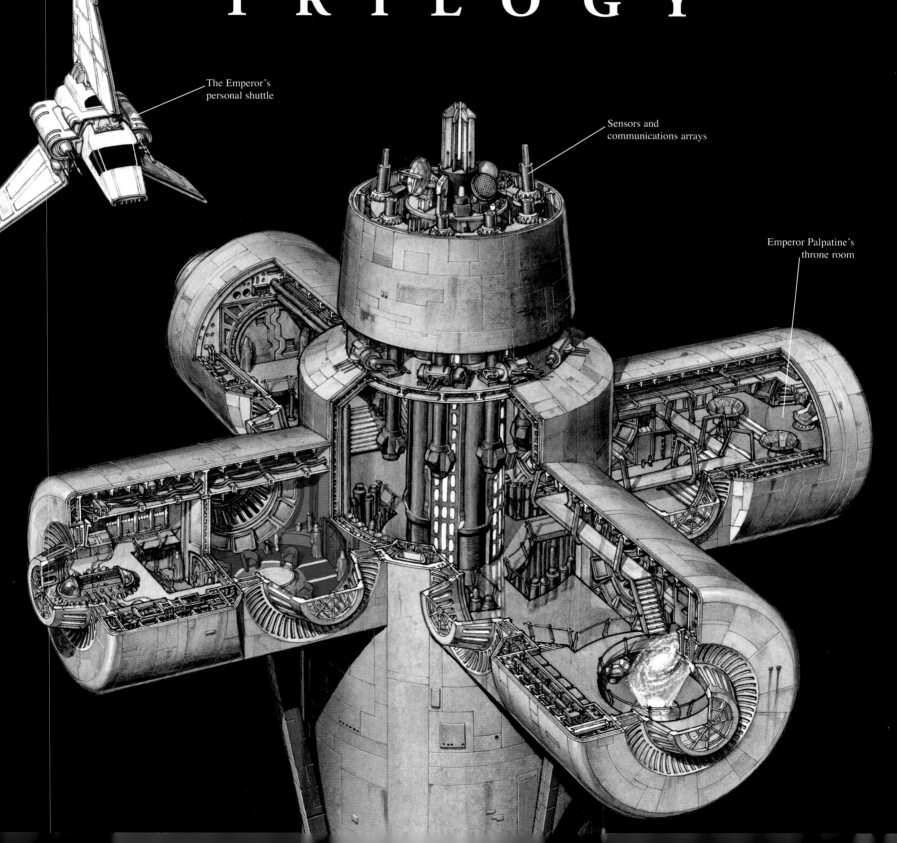

The Emperor's
personal shuttle

Sensors and
communications arrays

Emperor Palpatine's
throne room

INSIDE THE WORLDS OF

STAR WARS®

TRILOGY

Written by
James Luceno

Consultant
Curtis Saxton

Illustrated by
Richard Chasemore and Hans Jenssen

Additional illustrations by
Robert E. Barnes, John Mullaney, Richard Bonson, and Jon Hall

www.starwars.com   LUCAS BOOKS   DK   www.dk.com

CONTENTS

INTRODUCTION
5

TATOOINE
6

LARS HOMESTEAD
8

TOSCHE STATION / BEN'S HOUSE
10

MOS EISLEY
12

THE CANTINA
14

THE DEATH STAR
16

THE GREAT TEMPLE
18

BATTLE OF HOTH
20

ECHO BASE
22

DAGOBAH
26

YODA'S HOUSE
28

CLOUD CITY
30

PROCESSING VANE
32

JABBA'S PALACE
34

JABBA'S THRONE ROOM
36

BATTLE OF ENDOR
38

EWOK VILLAGE
40

DEATH STAR II
42

EMPEROR'S LAIR
44

EXECUTOR COMMAND TOWER
46

ACKNOWLEDGEMENTS
48

INTRODUCTION

Y EARS OF IMPERIAL RULE has left no corner of the galaxy untouched by civil war. Many key events of the rebellion transpire in the most improbable places: on the frozen wastes of ice-bound planets and in the murky swamps of jungle worlds; in the gleaming corridors of floating cities and starships; inside ancient temples, seedy cantinas, primitive treetop villages, and the grim throne rooms of crime lords. There is no Jedi High Council to spearhead the cause of peace and justice—only the children of a Jedi Knight who turned to the dark side, their motley fellowship of rogues and scoundrels, and a ragtag force comprised of former Senators, defectors, and slaves. Challenging them are the awesome war machines of the Empire, a merciless, unfeeling dictatorship—and the Emperor's twisted minion, Darth Vader, in whose hands the fate of the galaxy has rested since he was a young slave on the lawless planet called Tatooine.

TATOOINE

Distance from Core:	43,000 light-years
Number of Suns:	2
Number of Moons:	3
Population:	200,000 (humans, Jawas, Sand People, Hutts, and other species)
Surface Water:	1%
Composition:	Molten core with rocky mantle and silicate rock crust

A desert world located in the Arkanis sector of the Outer Rim, TATOOINE is thought to be one of oldest planets in known space. Fossils bear testament to an ocean-covered formative period, although today Tatooine is all but waterless.

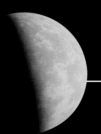

YAVIN 4

Distance from Core:	40,500 light-years
Number of Suns:	1
Number of Moons:	0
Population:	Fewer than 10 (after evacuation of Rebel Alliance base)
Surface Water:	8%
Composition:	Molten metallic core with thick, immobile, low-relief silicate crust

The largest of 13 moons orbiting the giant gas-planet Yavin, YAVIN 4 is distinguished by interconnected continents and inland seas. Turbulent rivers plunge from volcanic heights to meander through endless tracts of pristine jungle. Here, the purple-barked Massassi tree thrives, named for the ancient civilization that once inhabited the moon and that left behind towering stone monuments. Yavin 4 has extreme wet and dry seasons, the former of which often gives rise to violent storms.

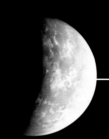

The sixth planet in a system of the same name, HOTH is an isolated, desolate, ice-bound globe that circles a blue-white sun. It is also a perpetual target for meteors spun off from a nearby asteroid field. Daylight temperatures rarely exceed freezing point, even in Hoth's relatively temperate equatorial zone, and much lower readings are not uncommon at night. One third of Hoth consists of open ocean, and the remainder is either ice-covered continents or sea areas under ice shelves. The planet's massive glaciers are riddled with caverns, and crystalline geysers punctuate the frigid surface.

HOTH

Distance from Core:	50, 250 light-years
Number of Suns:	1
Number of Moons:	3
Population:	Fewer than 10 (after evacuation of Rebel Alliance base)
Surface Water:	100% (mostly frozen)
Composition:	Molten metallic core with dichotomous crust and nearly global ice caps

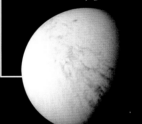

DAGOBAH

Distance from Core:	50,250 light-years
Number of Suns:	1
Number of Moons:	0
Population:	1 known sentient
Surface Water:	Approx. 8% in lakes and inland seas (muddy areas much more extensive)
Composition:	Molten metallic core with thick, immobile, low-relief silicate crust

Mysterious, mist-shrouded DAGOBAH in the remote Sluis sector has neither cities nor an indigenous population of sentients. Rather, the near fabled swamp planet is a veritable cauldron of life, brimming with exotic fauna and flora, such as the gnarltree, which begins its life as a species of spider, and then grows to such size that its buttressed roots fashion themselves into enchanted living caves. Dagobah's continental and oceanic crusts are only vaguely defined, and there is little in the way of volcanic activity or earthquakes. The surface is relatively flat, with water distributed in countless shallow lakes and lagoons.

BESPIN

Distance from Core:	49,100 light-years
Number of Suns:	1
Number of Moons:	2 principal (numerous unremarkable others)
Population:	6 million (humanoids and Ugnaughts)
Surface Water:	None
Composition:	Solid metal and silicate core; thick layers of liquid-metallic rethen; gaseous atmosphere

BESPIN is one of the few gas giants in the galaxy that is capable of harboring a wide variety of life. Separated from its two sister worlds by an asteroid belt known as Velser's Ring, the planet rotates every 12 standard-hours, orbits its sun every 14 standard-years, and is a primary source of naturally occurring tibanna gas. Bespin has no landmasses, but its upper atmosphere of billowing clouds hosts an envelope of breathable air, within which float exquisite orbital cities and sleek gas-mining facilities.

ENDOR

Distance from Core:	43,300 light-years
Number of Suns:	2
Number of Moons:	0
Population:	30 million (principally ewoks, yuzzum, and goraxes)
Surface Water:	8%
Composition:	Molten metallic core with thick, immobile, low-relief silicate crust

Largest of the nine moons of a gas giant in the inaccessible Moddell sector, ENDOR—known variously as the Sanctuary or Forest Moon—is a temperate world of woodlands, savannas, and mountain ranges. Many native life-forms thrive in Endor's relatively light gravity and hospitable climate.

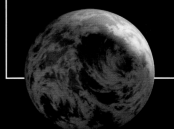

TATOOINE

INHABITABLE ONLY in one small area of its northern hemisphere, Tatooine is as rugged and desolate a planet as exists anywhere in the galaxy's Outer Rim. Baked by day, near frozen at night, the desert world might never have been colonized by humans had its ancient sea beds not dangled the promise of mineral wealth to a few desperate settlers from the Core willing to bet their lives on a lucky strike. With massacres and swindling, Tatooine's indigenous Sand People and Jawas were the first to warn the newcomers not to get their hopes up. But still they came. Pilfering from the parched air what little moisture there was, the farmers grew more hardened and embittered with each passing generation; accepting of the smugglers, slave traders, and outlaws who followed in their wake, they finally became resigned to lives of adversity.

8 Returning to Tatooine to save Han Solo from Jabba the Hutt, Luke Skywalker, now a Jedi Knight, is captured and forced to walk the plank over the Pit of Carkoon, lair of the insatiable sarlacc. Luke prepares to catch the lightsaber R2-D2 will propel to him from the deck of Jabba's sail barge.

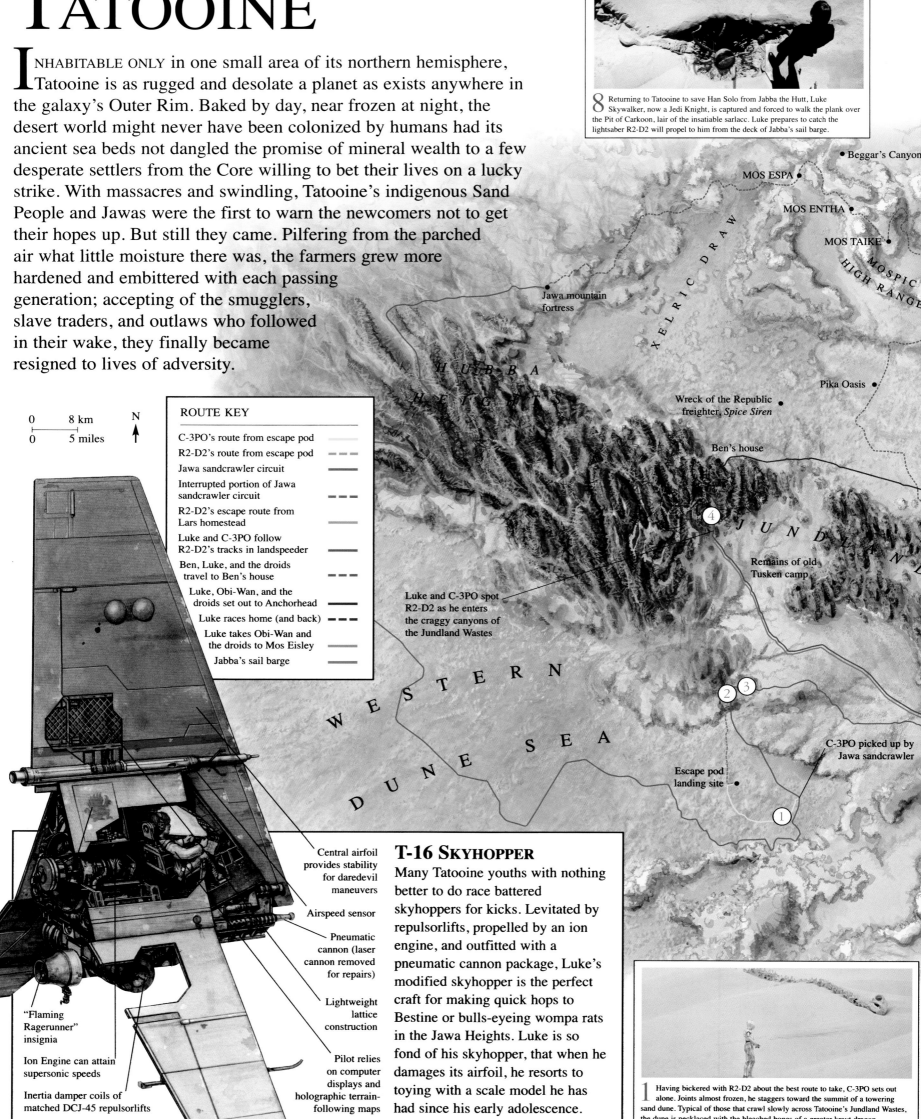

0	8 km	N
0	5 miles	↑

ROUTE KEY

C-3PO's route from escape pod	
R2-D2's route from escape pod	
Jawa sandcrawler circuit	
Interrupted portion of Jawa sandcrawler circuit	
R2-D2's escape route from Lars homestead	
Luke and C-3PO follow R2-D2's tracks in landspeeder	
Ben, Luke, and the droids travel to Ben's house	
Luke, Obi-Wan, and the droids set out to Anchorhead	
Luke races home (and back)	
Luke takes Obi-Wan and the droids to Mos Eisley	
Jabba's sail barge	

Beggar's Canyon

MOS ESPA

MOS ENTHA

MOS TAIKE

MOSPIC HIGH RANGE

XELRIC DRAW

Jawa mountain fortress

HUBBA HEIGHTS

Pika Oasis

Wreck of the Republic freighter, *Spice Siren*

Ben's house

JUNDLAND

Remains of old Tusken camp

Luke and C-3PO spot R2-D2 as he enters the craggy canyons of the Jundland Wastes

WESTERN DUNE SEA

C-3PO picked up by Jawa sandcrawler

Escape pod landing site

T-16 SKYHOPPER

Many Tatooine youths with nothing better to do race battered skyhoppers for kicks. Levitated by repulsorlifts, propelled by an ion engine, and outfitted with a pneumatic cannon package, Luke's modified skyhopper is the perfect craft for making quick hops to Bestine or bulls-eyeing wompa rats in the Jawa Heights. Luke is so fond of his skyhopper, that when he damages its airfoil, he resorts to toying with a scale model he has had since his early adolescence.

Central airfoil provides stability for daredevil maneuvers

Airspeed sensor

Pneumatic cannon (laser cannon removed for repairs)

Lightweight lattice construction

Pilot relies on computer displays and holographic terrain-following maps

"Flaming Ragerunner" insignia

Ion Engine can attain supersonic speeds

Inertia damper coils of matched DCJ-45 repulsorlifts

1 Having bickered with R2-D2 about the best route to take, C-3PO sets out alone. Joints almost frozen, he staggers toward the summit of a towering sand dune. Typical of those that crawl slowly across Tatooine's Jundland Wastes, the dune is necklaced with the bleached bones of a greater krayt dragon.

7 Rejoining Obi-Wan and the droids, Luke speeds to Mos Eisley, stopping only briefly to gaze on the spaceport from a steep-sided bluff. While Mos Eisley is the group's best chance of finding safe transport off Tatooine, they will have to be cautious, Obi-Wan warns, because the city teems with thieves and villains.

SoroSuub X-34 Landspeeder

Landspeeders are standard personal transports on Tatooine. Although superseded by the XP-38, SoroSuub's "Thirty-four" is still considered a classic because of its no-frill design and powerful engine. Even without modifications, the X-34 can attain top speeds of 250 kilometers (155 miles) per hour, and is highly maneuverable in tight quarters.

Top engine fuel lines
Combustion chamber
Power generator
Anti-grav generator
Service access panel
Duraplex windscreen
Fuel filler cap
Fuel Tank
Forward scanner
Repulsor anti-grav conduit
Port engine fuel lines
Repulsor elements

Map labels

NORTHERN DUNE SEA

BANTHA PLAINS

Jabba's Palace •

Site of Tusken slaughter by bandit Alkhara

B'OMARR FLATS

Pit of Carkoon ⑧

Stormtroopers charged with finding the missing droids intercept the Jawa sandcrawler as it leaves Bestine

On the journey to Mos Eisley, Ben, Luke and the droids shelter overnight in Bestine

GREAT MESRA PLATEAU

BESTINE

Bildor's Canyon

ARNTHOUT

⑦

MOS EISLEY

Wreck of the pirate vessel, *Hydian Marauder*

WASTES

Sluuce Canyon is well-used route to Mos Eisley valley from high ground

Rumored location of Kitonak Colony

Wreck of the Hutt transport, *Rimrunner*

Motesta Oasis

Jawa Heights •

Darklighter homestead

ANCHORHEAD

Tosche Station

⑥

Lars Homestead

GREAT CHOTT SALT FLAT COMMUNITY

6 Hurrying home, Luke discovers that the Lars farm has been burned, along with the bodies of his foster parents, Uncle Owen and Aunt Beru. His own life suddenly reduced to ashes, the grief-stricken youth resolves to learn the ways of the Force and to become a Jedi—like his father.

5 Revived by Obi-Wan from the blows of a Tusken gaffi stick, Luke offers Ben a landspeeder ride to the settlement of Anchorhead. Along the way, they chance upon a crippled sandcrawler and its Jawa crew, who have been massacred by Imperial troops, possibly in search of the droids.

Desert Dangers

With its vast unpopulated stretches of rock and sand, its primitive surface roads, and the unlighted alleyways of its principal settlements, Tatooine offers ample opportunities for personal misfortune. For sentients and droids alike, safety is as scarce as water, and banditry, abduction, and hijacking have been raised to art forms. Casual travelers risk being shot at by Tusken Raiders. Moisture farmers are frequently robbed of their profits by gangs of outlaws. And a lone droid need always be fearful of being abducted by Jawas. Tatooine's local authorities are too overwhelmed to deal with petty crime, and the troops of the Imperial garrison couldn't care less.

2 With suns-set, Tatooine's temperatures plunge, the darkened rocky canyons fill with unsettling sounds, and even R2-D2 is forced to reconsider his route. Stunned to immobility by an ionization blaster fired by a Jawa, the astromech is carried off by a group of these entrepreneurial beings, led by Dathcha.

3 On the hazy horizon, reflected sunlight glints off the thick bow-plating of a massive sandcrawler. Once used by ore-prospecting colonists, then abandoned to the wastes, the steam-powered transports are now piloted by clans of tech-scavenging Jawas, ever on the alert for abandoned or disoriented merchandise.

4 The two droids wind up as possessions of the moisture-farming Lars family. Under cover of darkness, however, R2-D2 escapes the compound, setting out for Obi-Wan Kenobi. The next morning, Luke pursues with C-3PO—only to be waylaid by a band of vicious Tusken Raiders.

LARS HOMESTEAD

SHADOWS SHORTEN as Tatooine's twin suns climb high above the Jundland Wastes, whose southern extreme is home to the several dozen moisture farms that make up the Great Chott salt flat community. Founded in the waning days of the Galactic Republic by Cliegg Lars and bequeathed to his son, Owen, the underground homestead is a warren of interconnected rooms, with vast storage areas and a marginally profitable hydroponic garden. Baked by the midday heat and scoured by gritty winds, the farm's pourstone entry dome and scattered moisture vaporators are the only exceptions to the glaring monotony of the desiccated seabed.

Luke brings up the difficult question of when he can join the Academy—unaware that his life is soon to change for ever.

TYPICAL FARMSTEAD

Ringed by rudimentary weather monitors and motion-detection sensors, the farm sprawls across a bleached expanse of low ridges and hard-packed ground. Many of the homestead's sand-pitted moisture vaporators are decades old and in need of almost-constant maintenance. Desperate to conserve power from solar radiation and small fusion-cell generators, the compound is shut down at nightfall—except for perimeter security sensors, which warn of roaming Tuskens and desert monsters.

Storage room for emergency rations and medical supplies is frequent haunt for womp rats

Dining room furniture originally supplied by mining company

Cup of nutrient-enhanced blue milk

Beru Whitesun Lars sets the dining room table for lunch

Coolth unit

Blue milk dispenser

Galley kitchen

Shape-memory, self-sealing containers and quick-prep devices prevent food from losing moisture to dry air

Compost-capable refresher unit

Combination water and sonic shower

Low-yield, flow-regulated wash basin

Refresher station

EG-6 power droid is several hundred years old

Pipes deliver water throughout homestead

Binary brain unit

Vaporator moisture condenser, or chilling bar

Water-filled cistern adjusts PH levels

Patch-in droid unit can converse with vaporator in binary language code

Wed 15 "Septoid 2" Treadwell toolkit droid sometimes chases sandflies, mistaking their whine for malfunctioning vaporators

Air intake/exhaust vanes control temperature in hydroponics chamber

Fusion-generator supply tanks

Laced with traces of magnetic ore, hardpacked soil serves as insulator from daytime heat and nighttime chill

Electrostatic repeller keeps courtyard and room entrances free of blowing sand

Training datapad for Imperial Academy

Humidity sensor controls air-moisture levels in hydroponics chamber

Owen Lars emerges from storage area with replacement parts for power converters

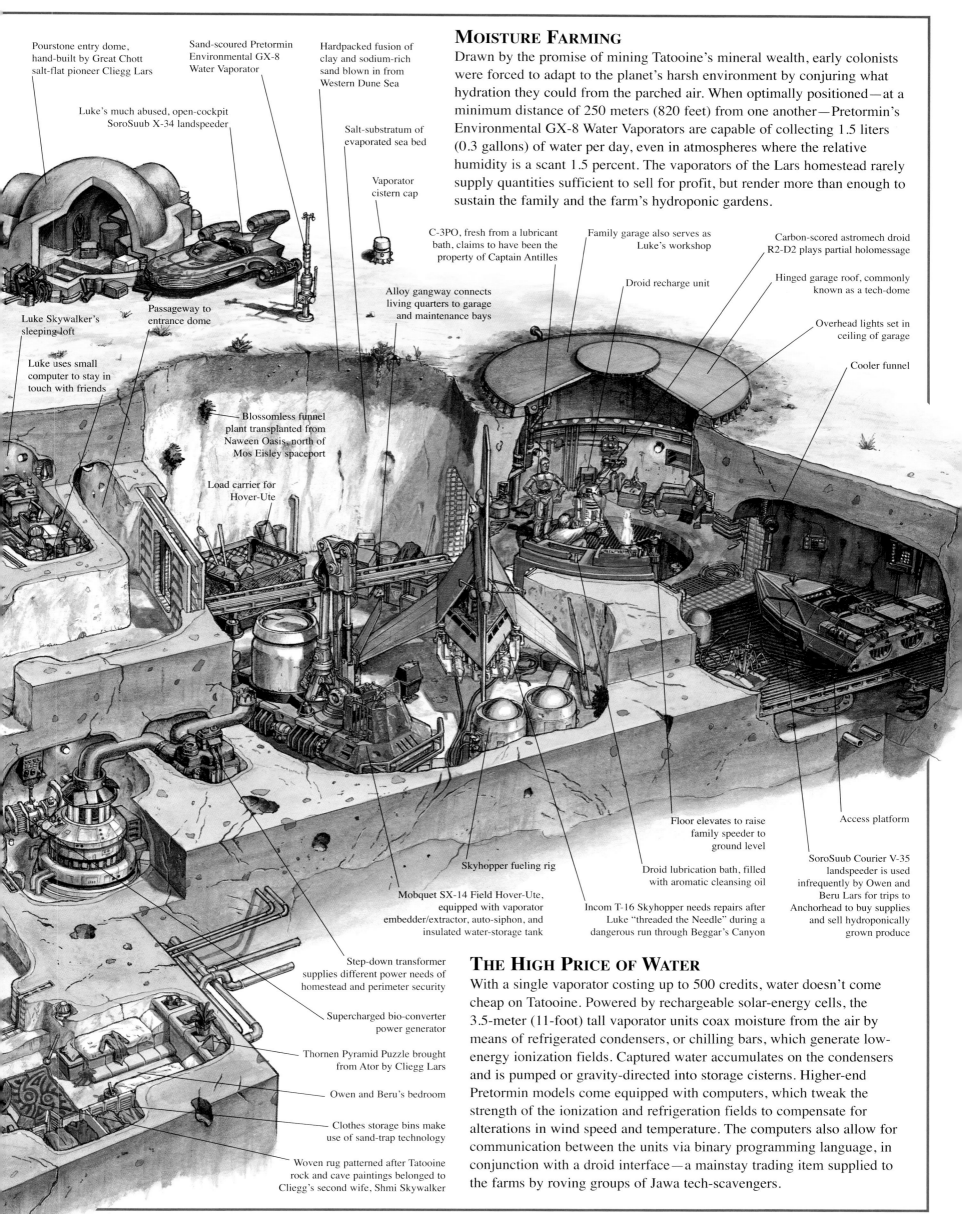

Pourstone entry dome, hand-built by Great Chott salt-flat pioneer Cliegg Lars

Sand-scoured Pretormin Environmental GX-8 Water Vaporator

Hardpacked fusion of clay and sodium-rich sand blown in from Western Dune Sea

MOISTURE FARMING

Drawn by the promise of mining Tatooine's mineral wealth, early colonists were forced to adapt to the planet's harsh environment by conjuring what hydration they could from the parched air. When optimally positioned—at a minimum distance of 250 meters (820 feet) from one another—Pretormin's Environmental GX-8 Water Vaporators are capable of collecting 1.5 liters (0.3 gallons) of water per day, even in atmospheres where the relative humidity is a scant 1.5 percent. The vaporators of the Lars homestead rarely supply quantities sufficient to sell for profit, but render more than enough to sustain the family and the farm's hydroponic gardens.

Luke's much abused, open-cockpit SoroSuub X-34 landspeeder

Salt-substratum of evaporated sea bed

Vaporator cistern cap

C-3PO, fresh from a lubricant bath, claims to have been the property of Captain Antilles

Family garage also serves as Luke's workshop

Carbon-scored astromech droid R2-D2 plays partial holomessage

Droid recharge unit

Hinged garage roof, commonly known as a tech-dome

Luke Skywalker's sleeping loft

Passageway to entrance dome

Overhead lights set in ceiling of garage

Luke uses small computer to stay in touch with friends

Alloy gangway connects living quarters to garage and maintenance bays

Cooler funnel

Blossomless funnel plant transplanted from Naween Oasis, north of Mos Eisley spaceport

Load carrier for Hover-Ute

Floor elevates to raise family speeder to ground level

Access platform

Skyhopper fueling rig

Droid lubrication bath, filled with aromatic cleansing oil

SoroSuub Courier V-35 landspeeder is used infrequently by Owen and Beru Lars for trips to Anchorhead to buy supplies and sell hydroponically grown produce

Mobquet SX-14 Field Hover-Ute, equipped with vaporator embedder/extractor, auto-siphon, and insulated water-storage tank

Incom T-16 Skyhopper needs repairs after Luke "threaded the Needle" during a dangerous run through Beggar's Canyon

Step-down transformer supplies different power needs of homestead and perimeter security

THE HIGH PRICE OF WATER

With a single vaporator costing up to 500 credits, water doesn't come cheap on Tatooine. Powered by rechargeable solar-energy cells, the 3.5-meter (11-foot) tall vaporator units coax moisture from the air by means of refrigerated condensers, or chilling bars, which generate low-energy ionization fields. Captured water accumulates on the condensers and is pumped or gravity-directed into storage cisterns. Higher-end Pretormin models come equipped with computers, which tweak the strength of the ionization and refrigeration fields to compensate for alterations in wind speed and temperature. The computers also allow for communication between the units via binary programming language, in conjunction with a droid interface—a mainstay trading item supplied to the farms by roving groups of Jawa tech-scavengers.

Supercharged bio-converter power generator

Thornen Pyramid Puzzle brought from Ator by Cliegg Lars

Owen and Beru's bedroom

Clothes storage bins make use of sand-trap technology

Woven rug patterned after Tatooine rock and cave paintings belonged to Cliegg's second wife, Shmi Skywalker

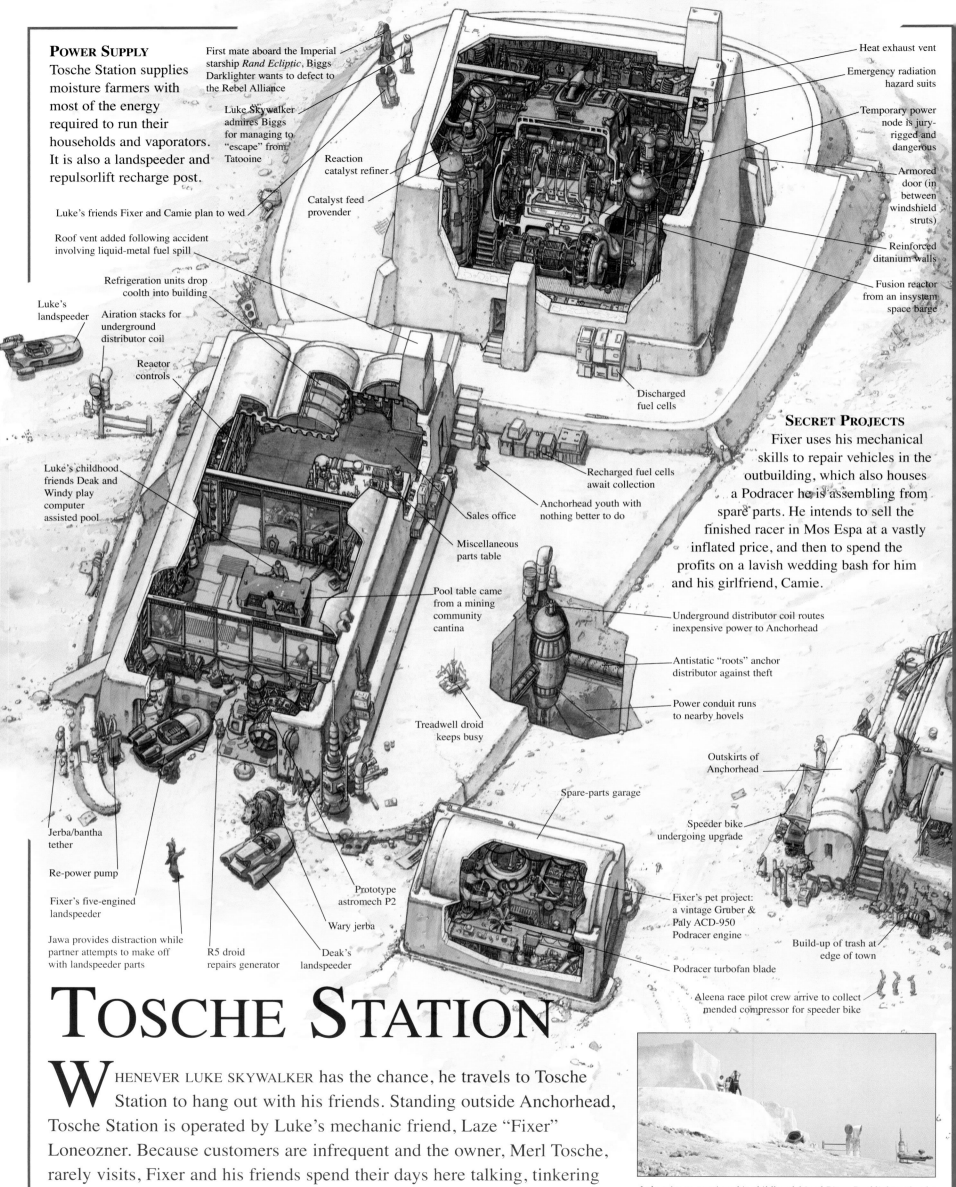

POWER SUPPLY
Tosche Station supplies moisture farmers with most of the energy required to run their households and vaporators. It is also a landspeeder and repulsorlift recharge post.

First mate aboard the Imperial starship *Rand Ecliptic*, Biggs Darklighter wants to defect to the Rebel Alliance

Luke Skywalker admires Biggs for managing to "escape" from Tatooine

Reaction catalyst refiner

Catalyst feed provender

Luke's friends Fixer and Camie plan to wed

Roof vent added following accident involving liquid-metal fuel spill

Refrigeration units drop coolth into building

Luke's landspeeder

Airation stacks for underground distributor coil

Reactor controls

Luke's childhood friends Deak and Windy play computer assisted pool

Heat exhaust vent

Emergency radiation hazard suits

Temporary power node is jury-rigged and dangerous

Armored door (in between windshield struts)

Reinforced ditanium walls

Fusion reactor from an insystem space barge

Discharged fuel cells

Recharged fuel cells await collection

Anchorhead youth with nothing better to do

Sales office

Miscellaneous parts table

Pool table came from a mining community cantina

SECRET PROJECTS
Fixer uses his mechanical skills to repair vehicles in the outbuilding, which also houses a Podracer he is assembling from spare parts. He intends to sell the finished racer in Mos Espa at a vastly inflated price, and then to spend the profits on a lavish wedding bash for him and his girlfriend, Camie.

Underground distributor coil routes inexpensive power to Anchorhead

Antistatic "roots" anchor distributor against theft

Power conduit runs to nearby hovels

Treadwell droid keeps busy

Outskirts of Anchorhead

Speeder bike undergoing upgrade

Jerba/bantha tether

Re-power pump

Fixer's five-engined landspeeder

Jawa provides distraction while partner attempts to make off with landspeeder parts

R5 droid repairs generator

Prototype astromech P2

Wary jerba

Deak's landspeeder

Spare-parts garage

Fixer's pet project: a vintage Gruber & Paly ACD-950 Podracer engine

Build-up of trash at edge of town

Podracer turbofan blade

Aleena race pilot crew arrive to collect mended compressor for speeder bike

TOSCHE STATION

WHENEVER LUKE SKYWALKER has the chance, he travels to Tosche Station to hang out with his friends. Standing outside Anchorhead, Tosche Station is operated by Luke's mechanic friend, Laze "Fixer" Loneozner. Because customers are infrequent and the owner, Merl Tosche, rarely visits, Fixer and his friends spend their days here talking, tinkering on their landspeeders and skyhoppers, and playing electronic pool.

Luke tries to convince his childhood friend Biggs Darklighter that he has witnessed a fierce battle taking place above Tatooine.

BEN'S HOUSE

Tatooine is dotted with remote dwellings built by those in search of profitable areas with higher-than-average nighttime condensation. Typically, these frontier moisture farmers return to safer and more populous areas after a single harsh season. One such abandoned dwelling, constructed over a well-sheltered cave, became the home of a Jedi Knight in hiding—Obi-Wan "Ben" Kenobi.

Ben's home is located on a remote bluff in the Jundland Wastes, surrounded on all sides by the Western Dune Sea. The nearest settlement is Bestine.

BASIC HOME

Ben Kenobi's simple house consists of one main room in which he lives and sleeps. He uses the natural cellar for food and water storage, and constructs mechanical items, for trading with Jawas, on a workbench.

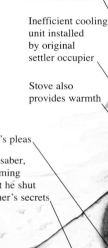

Damage to landspeeder jet-engine nacelle caused by Tusken attack

Luke Skywalker and Ben Kenobi view Princess Leia's pleas

After seeing Anakin's lightsaber, C-3PO's protocol programming requires him to request that he shut down to protect his ex-owner's secrets

Ben's couch doubles as a bed

Coolth dispersed into room below

Inefficient cooling unit installed by original settler occupier

Stove also provides warmth

Typical Tatooine pourstone roof dome

Coolth pump

Refresher station

Leeches and ropes

Ventilation chimney

Low-output moisture vaporator

Ritual bladed weapons taken from Sand People

Grapple and antique rifle

Jedi robe resembles simple clothing worn by species throughout galaxy

Found artefacts from Tatooine pre-history

Jerba-skin rug

Vacuum-seal chest contains Anakin Skywalker's lightsaber, which Obi-Wan had been waiting to give to Luke

Hidden trap door to cellar

Plasteel door

Bottles of cactus pulque

Stairs hewn from bedrock

Auxiliary generator

Heater for cold desert nights

MEAGRE EXISTENCE

This ageing Jedi spends most days meditating and walking the remote canyons that make up the unrelenting surroundings. He has no vehicle, but occasionally rides into Mos Eisley in a Jawa sandcrawler to purchase provisions.

Water cistern

Fruits, vegetables, and meat hung to dry in pantry

Luminescent stone provides scant and eerie light

Starship acceleration chair serves as workroom swivel

Backpack contains survival gear and emergency rations

Workbench constructed from pieces of scrap metal

Key-pad safe box contains Kenobi's journal, with instructions for building a lightsaber

SORCERER'S REPUTATION

Obi-Wan sees few beings other than Jawas, from whom he obtains foodstuffs and spare parts—though his reputation as a wizard causes many Jawas, and even a few Sand People, to avoid him. There are some who—out of fear—present Old Ben with gifts intended to appease him.

MOS EISLEY

THE UNRULY SPACEPORT of Mos Eisley sprawls in a broad valley south-east of Tatooine's Jundland Wastes. The old quarter was originally laid out like a wheel, with a teeming market place located adjacent to water and power distribution centers. Now, bargains on vaporators, cooling units, and hydroponic produce can be found in the bazaars and junkyards of the newer quarter, the hub of which is Chalmun's Spaceport Cantina.

CITY-WIDE TRAFFIC

With no central landing area, the whole of Mos Eisley is cratered with 362 docking bays, many of which are large enough to accommodate space freighters. All the bays are under the ostensible control of the city prefect and a handful of overworked customs agents who answer to the commander of the city's small garrison of Imperial stormtroopers.

1 Luke Skywalker races toward Mos Eisley with Ben Kenobi, C-3PO, and R2-D2 crammed into his landspeeder. A slum of ramshackle pourstone buildings, the area is populated by squatters, failed moisture farmers, scavengers, and those outlaws who have come to Tatooine to lose or reinvent themselves.

2 Teams of ASP-7 droids assist in the loading of a Gallofree Yards, civilian-use GR-45 medium transport. Easily programmed and equipped with magnetized feet, clawed hands, and voice synthesizers, the agile droids will have the vessel's cargo-space loaded by suns-set.

3 Familiar with the layout of the city from previous visits, Obi-Wan directs Luke toward Chalmun's Cantina, on the far side of the city. Where Outer Curved Street and Straight Street intersect at the new city center, the skyline is dominated by hotels, casinos, and tall complexes built by off-planet corporations.

ONE CITY'S MISFORTUNE

Long a haven for spacers, thieves, smugglers, and rogues of all species and variety, Mos Eisley prides itself on being a wretched hive of scum and villainy. The spaceport's status swelled when Podracing fell out of favor, and slave traders and criminals like Jabba the Hutt abandoned that sport's epicenter to the north, Mos Espa. Jabba's increased presence attracted the notice of starship design corporations Ubrikkian and Queblux, both of which constructed high-rise buildings in the gentrified heart of the old city.

11 Having struck a sweet deal with Obi-Wan and Luke for passage to Alderaan, Han Solo finds Jabba the Hutt and his gang of mercenaries and bounty hunters waiting for him in Docking Bay 94. Han bargains with the Hutt for one final chance to pay for a load of spice he was forced to jettison.

Millennium Falcon makes a hasty exit

Hutt-owned exotic restaurant, Court of the Fountain

Former Podracer spare parts dealership

Passenger ship belonging to Roon Tours, which offers short vacations in Tatooine for wealthy, jaded tourists seeking unusual thrills

Overcrowded city jail

Illegally parked GR-45 medium transport

OUTER CURVED STREET

Spaceport Speeders, where Luke and Ben sell the family speeder

Docking Bay 94

Headquarters of Quebe-Luxfause Systems, manufacturers of queblux power technology

Water distribution plant

Spaceport Express

Masse Goskey's famous Arms Emporium

Entrance dome to Jabba the Hutt's townhouse, known as the Desilijic Complex, much of which is constructed over extensive system of caves and grottos

Jabba's private box

Jango Fett Arena (named in honor of the legendary bounty hunter) features all types of combat spectacles

SPACERS ROW

PARADISE ROAD

Many of Mos Eisley's citizens ride rontos, jerbas, dewbacks, and other beasts

Though few Neimoidians travel far after Clone Wars, their shuttles are sometimes seen, especially when shady dealings are afoot

4 Luke maneuver the landspeeder into Straight Street toward what was once the heart of the Old City. As varied as the city's vehicles and droids, Mos Eisley's residents and transients have come to Tatooine from worlds as near as Ryloth and Piroket, and as distant as Nar Shaddaa and Ord Mantell.

5 Startled by a recklessly-piloted S-swoop, a ronto pack-beast rears up to avoid a collision, unseating his pair of Jawa riders. Animals such as rontos, banthas, dewbacks, jerbas, and eopies are as common a sight in Mos Eisley as landspeeders, skyhoppers, or arriving and departing spacecraft.

10 Renowned in Mos Eisley for his spying aptitude, a long-snouted alien from Kubindi, named Garindan, shadows Luke and Ben as they hastily sell their speeder in order to rendezvous with starship pilots Han Solo and Chewbacca at Docking Bay 94.

9 Partnered with Mark IV repulsorlift patrol droids and armed with BlasTech E-11, DLT-19, and T-21 repeating blasters, squads of stormtroopers search for the fugitive droids, sometimes resorting to house-to-house searches. C-3PO and R2-D2 are forced to hide in the maze of narrow streets to evade capture.

GALACTIC HOTSPOT

Moisture farmers bring their harvests to Mos Eisley only if markets in the capital of Bestine are overly busy. Notoriously open to bribes, customs officials make little attempt to curtail the smuggling of spice, illegal arms, and other proscribed goods that pass through Tatooine on their way to other worlds. Ben Kenobi makes occasional trips to Mos Eisley to learn the latest news about the Empire and the contemptible activities of his former apprentice, Anakin Skywalker—now Darth Vader.

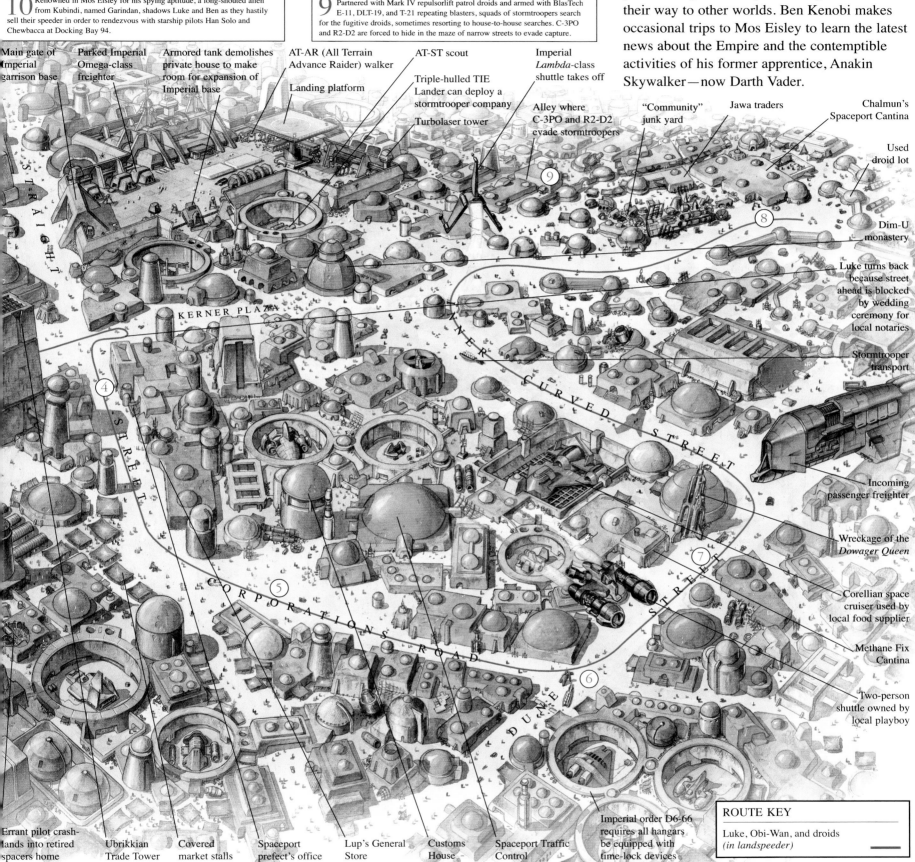

Main gate of Imperial garrison base

Parked Imperial Omega-class freighter

Armored tank demolishes private house to make room for expansion of Imperial base

AT-AR (All Terrain Advance Raider) walker

Landing platform

AT-ST scout

Triple-hulled TIE Lander can deploy a stormtrooper company

Turbolaser tower

Imperial *Lambda*-class shuttle takes off

Alley where C-3PO and R2-D2 evade stormtroopers

"Community" junk yard

Jawa traders

Chalmun's Spaceport Cantina

Used droid lot

Dim-U monastery

Luke turns back because street ahead is blocked by wedding ceremony for local notaries

Stormtrooper transport

Incoming passenger freighter

Wreckage of the *Dowager Queen*

Corellian space cruiser used by local food supplier

Methane Fix Cantina

Two-person shuttle owned by local playboy

STRAIGHT STREET

KERNER PLAZA

INNER CURVED STREET

CORPORATIONS ROAD

DUNE STREET

Errant pilot crash-lands into retired spacers home

Ubrikkian Trade Tower

Covered market stalls

Spaceport prefect's office

Lup's General Store

Customs House

Spaceport Traffic Control

Imperial order D6-66 requires all hangars be equipped with time-lock devices

ROUTE KEY

Luke, Obi-Wan, and droids *(in landspeeder)*

6 At a checkpoint set up by a contingent of sandtroopers, Ben employs a Jedi mind trick to persuade the weak-willed Imperial clone soldiers that they don't need to ascertain his or Luke's identity or establish just how long they have owned the pair of droids.

7 The early colony ship *Dowager Queen* towers above a sprawl of low domes and crater-like landing bays. The upended spaceship is one of many that have crashed on the surface of the planet and become either local landmarks or occupied structures in Mos Eisley.

8 While Luke and Obi-Wan attempt to seek out a skilled pilot with a fast ship, R2-D2 and C-3PO—having been ejected from Chalmun's Cantina—conceal themselves from a search party of stormtroopers by standing among a group of droids in a used droid lot nearby.

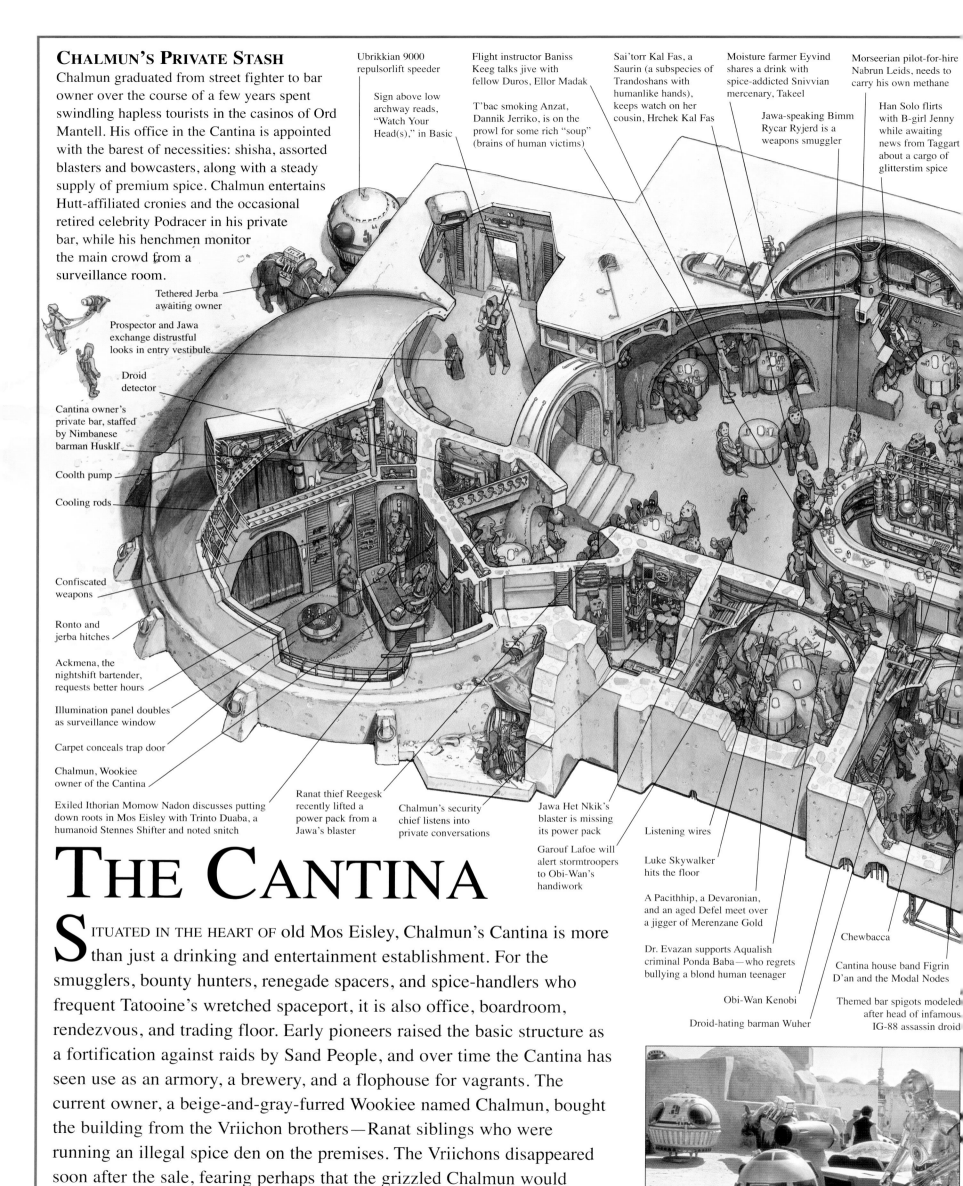

CHALMUN'S PRIVATE STASH

Chalmun graduated from street fighter to bar owner over the course of a few years spent swindling hapless tourists in the casinos of Ord Mantell. His office in the Cantina is appointed with the barest of necessities: shisha, assorted blasters and bowcasters, along with a steady supply of premium spice. Chalmun entertains Hutt-affiliated cronies and the occasional retired celebrity Podracer in his private bar, while his henchmen monitor the main crowd from a surveillance room.

Tethered Jerba awaiting owner

Prospector and Jawa exchange distrustful looks in entry vestibule

Droid detector

Cantina owner's private bar, staffed by Nimbanese barman Husklf

Coolth pump

Cooling rods

Confiscated weapons

Ronto and jerba hitches

Ackmena, the nightshift bartender, requests better hours

Illumination panel doubles as surveillance window

Carpet conceals trap door

Chalmun, Wookiee owner of the Cantina

Exiled Ithorian Momow Nadon discusses putting down roots in Mos Eisley with Trinto Duaba, a humanoid Stennes Shifter and noted snitch

Ranat thief Reegesk recently lifted a power pack from a Jawa's blaster

Chalmun's security chief listens into private conversations

Ubrikkian 9000 repulsorlift speeder

Sign above low archway reads, "Watch Your Head(s)," in Basic

Flight instructor Baniss Keeg talks jive with fellow Duros, Ellor Madak

T'bac smoking Anzat, Dannik Jerriko, is on the prowl for some rich "soup" (brains of human victims)

Sai'torr Kal Fas, a Saurin (a subspecies of Trandoshans with humanlike hands), keeps watch on her cousin, Hrchek Kal Fas

Moisture farmer Eyvind shares a drink with spice-addicted Snivvian mercenary, Takeel

Jawa-speaking Bimm Rycar Ryjerd is a weapons smuggler

Morseerian pilot-for-hire Nabrun Leids, needs to carry his own methane

Han Solo flirts with B-girl Jenny while awaiting news from Taggart about a cargo of glitterstim spice

Jawa Het Nkik's blaster is missing its power pack

Listening wires

Garouf Lafoe will alert stormtroopers to Obi-Wan's handiwork

Luke Skywalker hits the floor

A Pacithhip, a Devaronian, and an aged Defel meet over a jigger of Merenzane Gold

Dr. Evazan supports Aqualish criminal Ponda Baba—who regrets bullying a blond human teenager

Chewbacca

Cantina house band Figrin D'an and the Modal Nodes

Obi-Wan Kenobi

Droid-hating barman Wuher

Themed bar spigots modeled after head of infamous IG-88 assassin droid

THE CANTINA

SITUATED IN THE HEART OF old Mos Eisley, Chalmun's Cantina is more than just a drinking and entertainment establishment. For the smugglers, bounty hunters, renegade spacers, and spice-handlers who frequent Tatooine's wretched spaceport, it is also office, boardroom, rendezvous, and trading floor. Early pioneers raised the basic structure as a fortification against raids by Sand People, and over time the Cantina has seen use as an armory, a brewery, and a flophouse for vagrants. The current owner, a beige-and-gray-furred Wookiee named Chalmun, bought the building from the Vriichon brothers—Ranat siblings who were running an illegal spice den on the premises. The Vriichons disappeared soon after the sale, fearing perhaps that the grizzled Chalmun would discover the numerous bodies they had buried in the basement.

The droids wait outside the Cantina in the noon heat—Kenobi knows that this is the best time to find the bar crowded with thirsty starpilots.

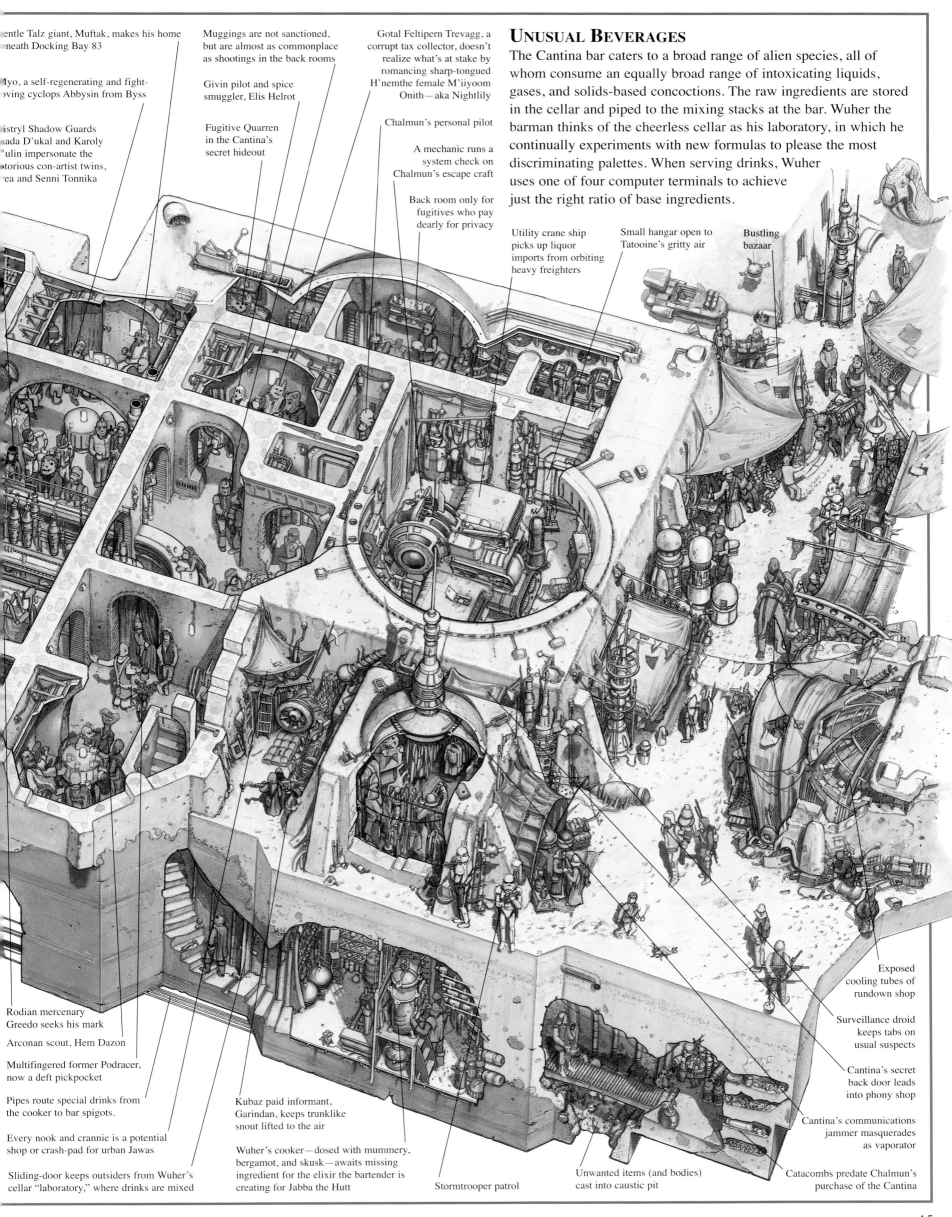

entle Talz giant, Muftak, makes his home
neath Docking Bay 83

Muggings are not sanctioned,
but are almost as commonplace
as shootings in the back rooms

Gotal Feltipern Trevagg, a
corrupt tax collector, doesn't
realize what's at stake by
romancing sharp-tongued
H'nemthe female M'iiyoom
Onith—aka Nightlily

Unusual Beverages

The Cantina bar caters to a broad range of alien species, all of
whom consume an equally broad range of intoxicating liquids,
gases, and solids-based concoctions. The raw ingredients are stored
in the cellar and piped to the mixing stacks at the bar. Wuher the
barman thinks of the cheerless cellar as his laboratory, in which he
continually experiments with new formulas to please the most
discriminating palettes. When serving drinks, Wuher
uses one of four computer terminals to achieve
just the right ratio of base ingredients.

Myo, a self-regenerating and fight-
oving cyclops Abbysin from Byss

Givin pilot and spice
smuggler, Elis Helrot

istryl Shadow Guards
ada D'ukal and Karoly
ulin impersonate the
torious con-artist twins,
ea and Senni Tonnika

Fugitive Quarren
in the Cantina's
secret hideout

Chalmun's personal pilot

A mechanic runs a
system check on
Chalmun's escape craft

Back room only for
fugitives who pay
dearly for privacy

Utility crane ship
picks up liquor
imports from orbiting
heavy freighters

Small hangar open to
Tatooine's gritty air

Bustling
bazaar

Rodian mercenary
Greedo seeks his mark

Arconan scout, Hem Dazon

Multifingered former Podracer,
now a deft pickpocket

Pipes route special drinks from
the cooker to bar spigots.

Every nook and crannie is a potential
shop or crash-pad for urban Jawas

Sliding-door keeps outsiders from Wuher's
cellar "laboratory," where drinks are mixed

Kubaz paid informant,
Garindan, keeps trunklike
snout lifted to the air

Wuher's cooker—dosed with mummery,
bergamot, and skusk—awaits missing
ingredient for the elixir the bartender is
creating for Jabba the Hutt

Stormtrooper patrol

Unwanted items (and bodies)
cast into caustic pit

Exposed
cooling tubes of
rundown shop

Surveillance droid
keeps tabs on
usual suspects

Cantina's secret
back door leads
into phony shop

Cantina's communications
jammer masquerades
as vaporator

Catacombs predate Chalmun's
purchase of the Cantina

15

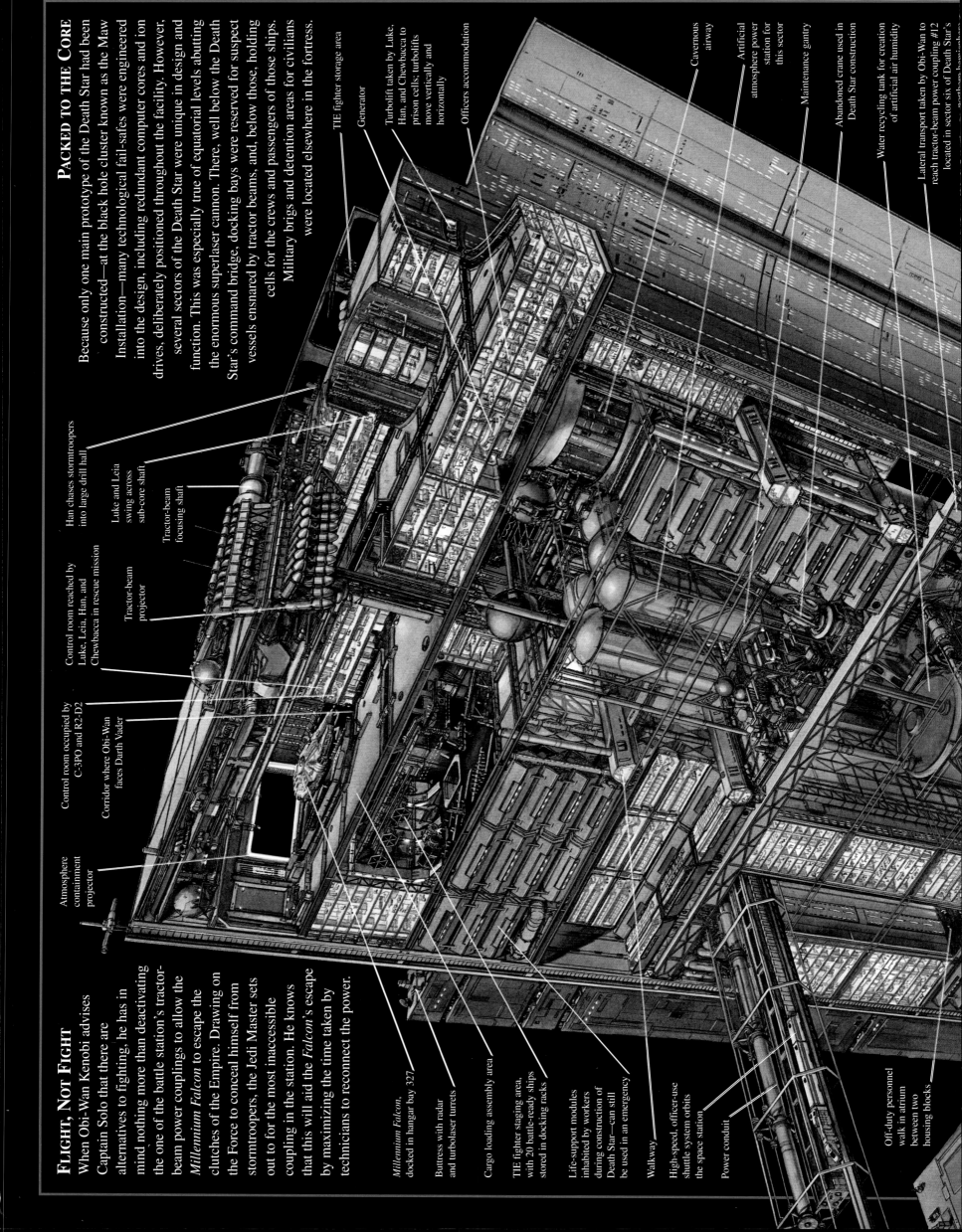

PACKED TO THE CORE

Because only one main prototype of the Death Star had been constructed—at the black hole cluster known as the Maw Installation—many technological fail-safes were engineered into the design, including redundant computer cores and ion drives, deliberately positioned throughout the facility. However, several sectors of the Death Star were unique in design and function. This was especially true of equatorial levels abutting the enormous superlaser cannon. There, well below the Death Star's command bridge, docking bays were reserved for suspect vessels ensnared by tractor beams, and, below those, holding cells for the crews and passengers of those ships. Military brigs and detention areas for civilians were located elsewhere in the fortress.

FLIGHT, NOT FIGHT

When Obi-Wan Kenobi advises Captain Solo that there are alternatives to fighting, he has in mind nothing more than deactivating the one of the battle station's tractor-beam power couplings to allow the *Millennium Falcon* to escape the clutches of the Empire. Drawing on the Force to conceal himself from stormtroopers, the Jedi Master sets out to for the most inaccessible coupling in the station. He knows that this will aid the *Falcon*'s escape by maximizing the time taken by technicians to reconnect the power.

Atmosphere containment projector

Control room occupied by C-3PO and R2-D2

Corridor where Obi-Wan faces Darth Vader

Control room reached by Luke, Leia, Han, and Chewbacca in rescue mission

Tractor-beam projector

Han chases stormtroopers into large drill hall

Luke and Leia swing across sub-core shaft

Tractor-beam focusing shaft

Millennium Falcon, docked in hangar bay 327

Buttress with radar and turbolaser turrets

Cargo loading assembly area

Life-support modules inhabited by workers during construction of Death Star—can still be used in an emergency

Walkway

High-speed, officer-use shuttle system orbits the space station

Power conduit

TIE fighter staging area, with 20 battle-ready ships stored in docking racks

TIE fighter storage area

Generator

Turbolift taken by Luke, Han, and Chewbacca to prison cells; turbolifts move vertically and horizontally

Officers accommodation

Cavernous airway

Artificial atmosphere power station for this sector

Maintenance gantry

Abandoned crane used in Death Star construction

Water recycling tank for creation of artificial air humidity

Lateral transport taken by Obi-Wan to reach tractor-beam power coupling #12 located in sector six of Death Star's

Off-duty personnel walk in atrium between two housing blocks

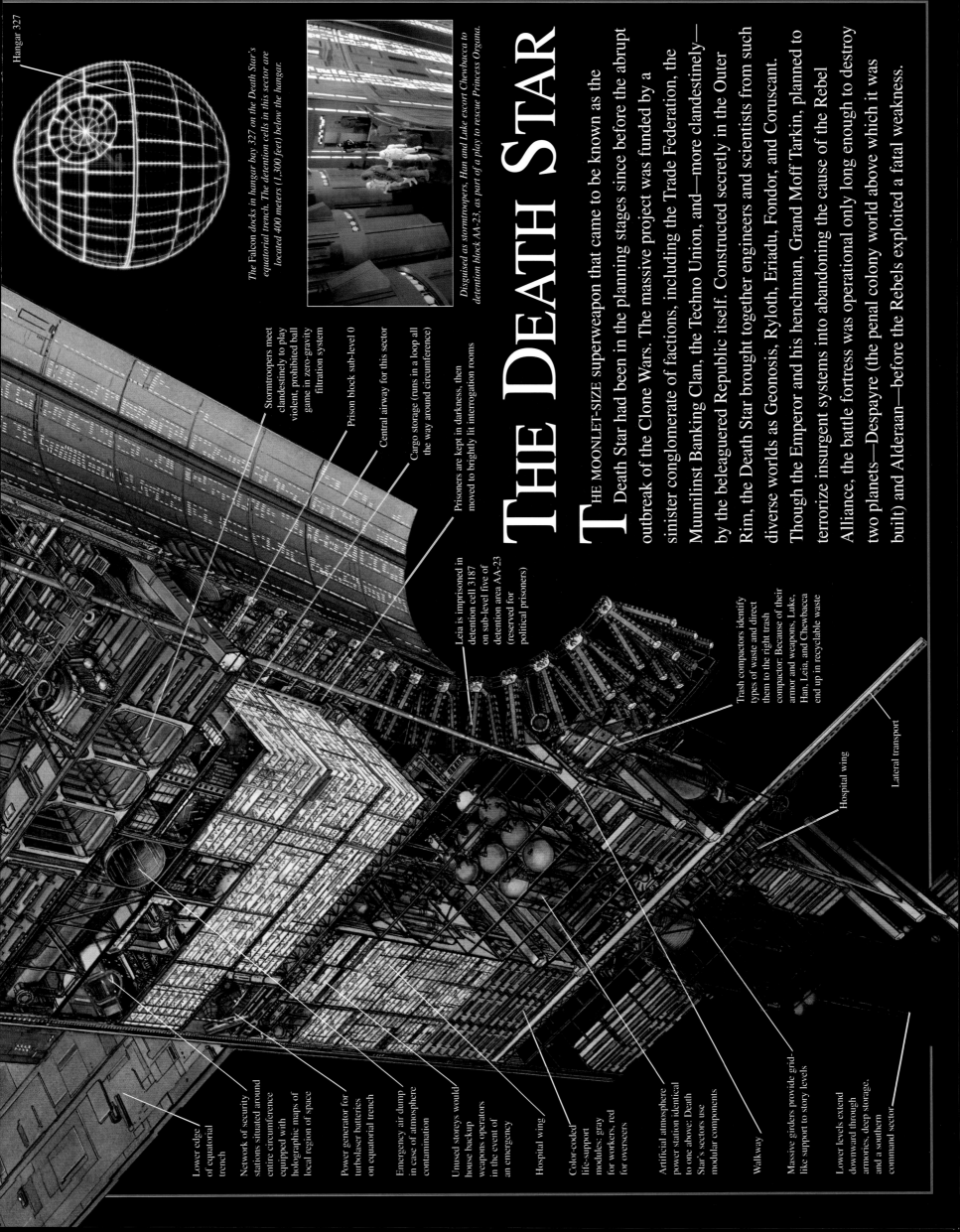

Hangar 327

The Falcon docks in hangar bay 327 on the Death Star's equatorial trench. The detention cells in this sector are located 400 meters (1,300 feet) below the hangar.

Disguised as stormtroopers, Han and Luke escort Chewbacca to detention block AA-23, as part of a play to rescue Princess Organa.

THE DEATH STAR

THE MOONLET-SIZE superweapon that came to be known as the Death Star had been in the planning stages since before the abrupt outbreak of the Clone Wars. The massive project was funded by a sinister conglomerate of factions, including the Trade Federation, the Muunilinst Banking Clan, the Techno Union, and—more clandestinely— by the beleaguered Republic itself. Constructed secretly in the Outer Rim, the Death Star brought together engineers and scientists from such diverse worlds as Geonosis, Ryloth, Eriadu, Fondor, and Coruscant. Though the Emperor and his henchman, Grand Moff Tarkin, planned to terrorize insurgent systems into abandoning the cause of the Rebel Alliance, the battle fortress was operational only long enough to destroy two planets—Despayre (the penal colony world above which it was built) and Alderaan—before the Rebels exploited a fatal weakness.

Stormtroopers meet clandestinely to play violent, prohibited ball game in zero-gravity filtration system

Prison block sub-level 0

Central airway for this sector

Cargo storage (runs in a loop all the way around circumference)

Prisoners are kept in darkness, then moved to brightly lit interrogation rooms

Leia is imprisoned in detention cell 3187 on sub-level five of detention area AA-23 (reserved for political prisoners)

Trash compactors identify types of waste and direct them to the right trash compactor. Because of their armor and weapons, Luke, Han, Leia, and Chewbacca end up in recyclable waste

Hospital wing

Lateral transport

Lower edge of equatorial trench

Network of security stations situated around entire circumference equipped with holographic maps of local region of space

Power generator for turbolaser batteries on equatorial trench

Emergency air dump in case of atmosphere contamination

Unused storeys would house backup weapons operators in the event of an emergency

Hospital wing

Color-coded life-support modules: gray for workers, red for overseers

Artificial atmosphere power station identical to one above: Death Star's sectors use modular components

Walkway

Massive girders provide grid-like support to story levels

Lower levels extend downward through armories, deep storage, and a southern command sector

THE GREAT TEMPLE

BLANKETED WITH NEARLY impenetrable vegetation, Yavin 4 is home to countless unique species of plants, animals, and insects, but hosts no intelligent lifeforms. The fourth moon of an uninhabitable gas giant, Yavin 4 had been of interest only to galactic archeologists, due to the ancient stone temples that rise majestically from its jungles. These towering, stepped structures are all that remain of the lost civilization of the Massassi. With no sentient population to subdue and no mineral wealth to exploit, Yavin 4 has been overlooked by the Empire and is seldom included on official maps. It was for precisely this reason that the resourceful leaders of the Rebel Alliance choose Yavin 4 as their base after having been forced to flee their previous command center on the planet Dantooine.

UNTAMED NATURE

The surrounding jungle of purple-barked Massassi trees resounds with the eerie cries and blood-chilling moans of unseen creatures: woolamanders, lizard crabs, stintaril rodents, and armored eels, among others. Dense thickets of thorny vegetation and unpredictable storms thwart the progress of surveyors and construction engineers. Thus, the Rebels stick to the laser-cut access and patrol routes that link the Great Temple to outlying landing zones and the distant power station.

MYSTERIOUS MASONS

The Massassi were a primitive warrior people who were enslaved by the Sith many millennia ago. About 5,000 years before the Battle of Yavin, an army of Massassi arrived on the moon with their leader, the Sith Dark Lord Naga Sadow, who was on the run after an unsuccessful bid for power. Though Sadow conducted cruel genetic experiments on his own troops—transforming the once-humanoid species into fearsome, hunchbacked predators—they treated him like a god, raising huge temples in his honor. Later archeologists proposed that the temples may have been large-scale communication devices that could reach Sith Lords across the galaxy.

POWER SUPPLY

The functioning of the base is reliant on a power-generating station located 1.2 miles (two kilometers) away. Pieced together from turbines and a main reactor stolen from an Imperial Star Destroyer, the station supplies sufficient power for a protective shield, ion cannons, and other defences that could hold off an assault from a single large battleship.

Having docked the Millennium Falcon at the nearby visitor landing zone, Luke, Han, Leia, and the droids are met by Rebel leaders outside the base's impregnable blast door.

Observation and communications room

Unknown to Rebels, roof comb was added by Dark Jedi Exar Kun for arcane power

Luke Skywalker, Han Solo, and Chewbacca march down aisle

Ceremony commemorating destruction of Death Star takes place in audience chamber

Princess Leia, General Dodonna, and other dignitaries stand on ceremonial podium

Holographic memorials to those killed in battle will be placed outside ceremonial hall

Central turbolift cluster

Roughly cut cavities drilled by rebels into straighter sides of original Massassi interior

Anti-personnel cannons

Auxiliary power generators

Temple built with no visible sign of advanced machinery

Back-up power plant

Briefing room

Tall skylights aligned with equinox and solstice

Turbolift to audience chamber

Massassi-built staircase to observation room at apex

Audience chamber floor tiled with translucent precious stones

Water reservoir

Command room

Barracks area for thousands of troops

Interior of temple clad with sheets of seamed metal

Algae, mosses, and vines resist Rebel attempts to blast original rock face clean of vegetation

Eight-sided pyramidal design echoes shape of Sith Holocrons

Thick blast door lowers to protect hangar bay

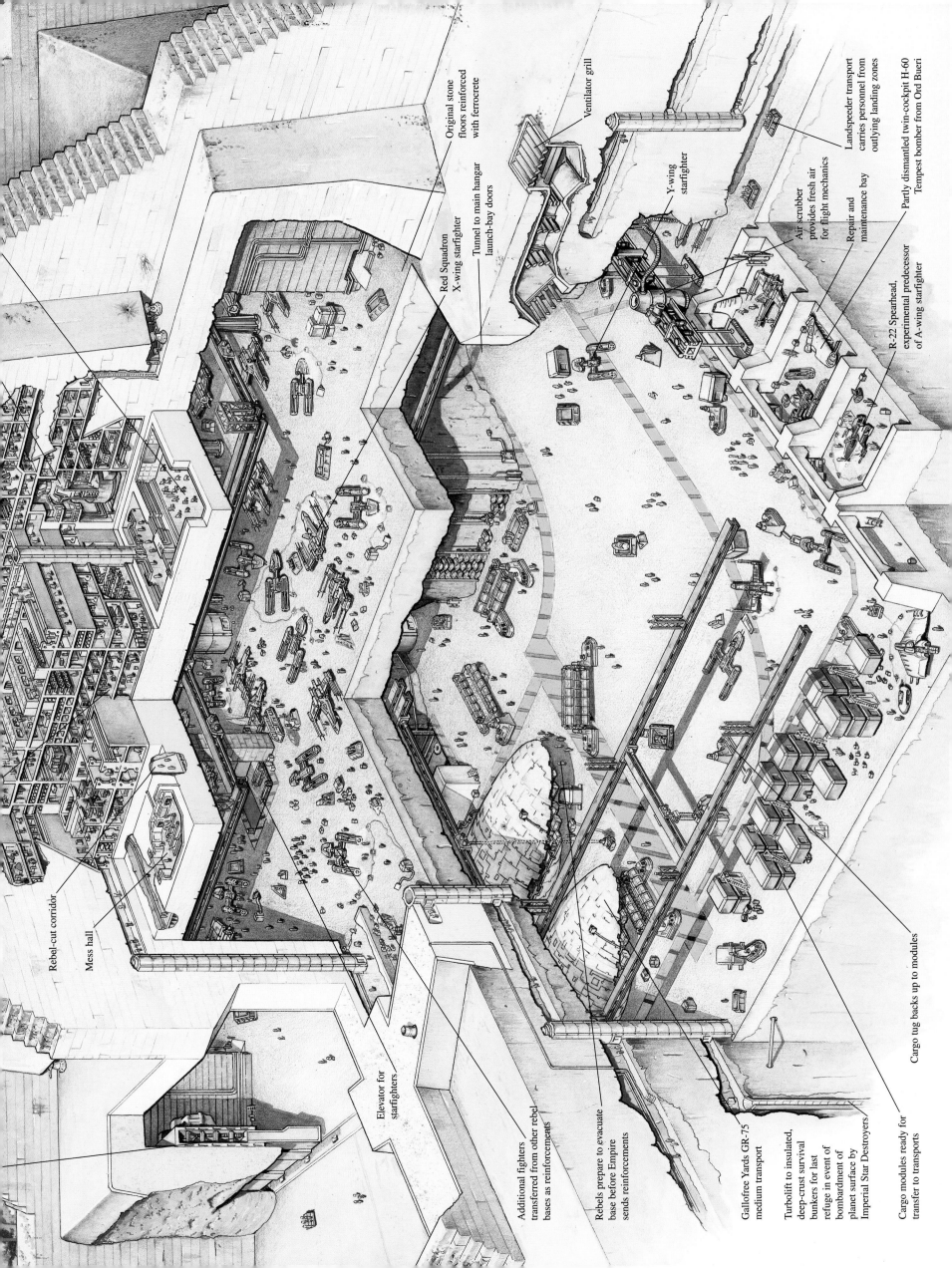

Original stone floors reinforced with ferrocrete

Ventilator grill

Landspeeder transport carries personnel from outlying landing zones

Y-wing starfighter

Air scrubber provides fresh air for flight mechanics

Repair and maintenance bay

Partly dismantled twin-cockpit H-60 Tempest bomber from Ord Bueri

Red Squadron X-wing starfighter

Tunnel to main hangar launch-bay doors

R-22 Spearhead, experimental predecessor of A-wing starfighter

Rebel-cut corridor

Mess hall

Elevator for starfighters

Additional fighters transferred from other rebel bases as reinforcements

Rebels prepare to evacuate base before Empire sends reinforcements

Gallofree Yards GR-75 medium transport

Turbolift to insulated, deep-crust survival bunkers for last refuge in event of bombardment of planet surface by Imperial Star Destroyers

Cargo modules ready for transfer to transports

Cargo tug backs up to modules

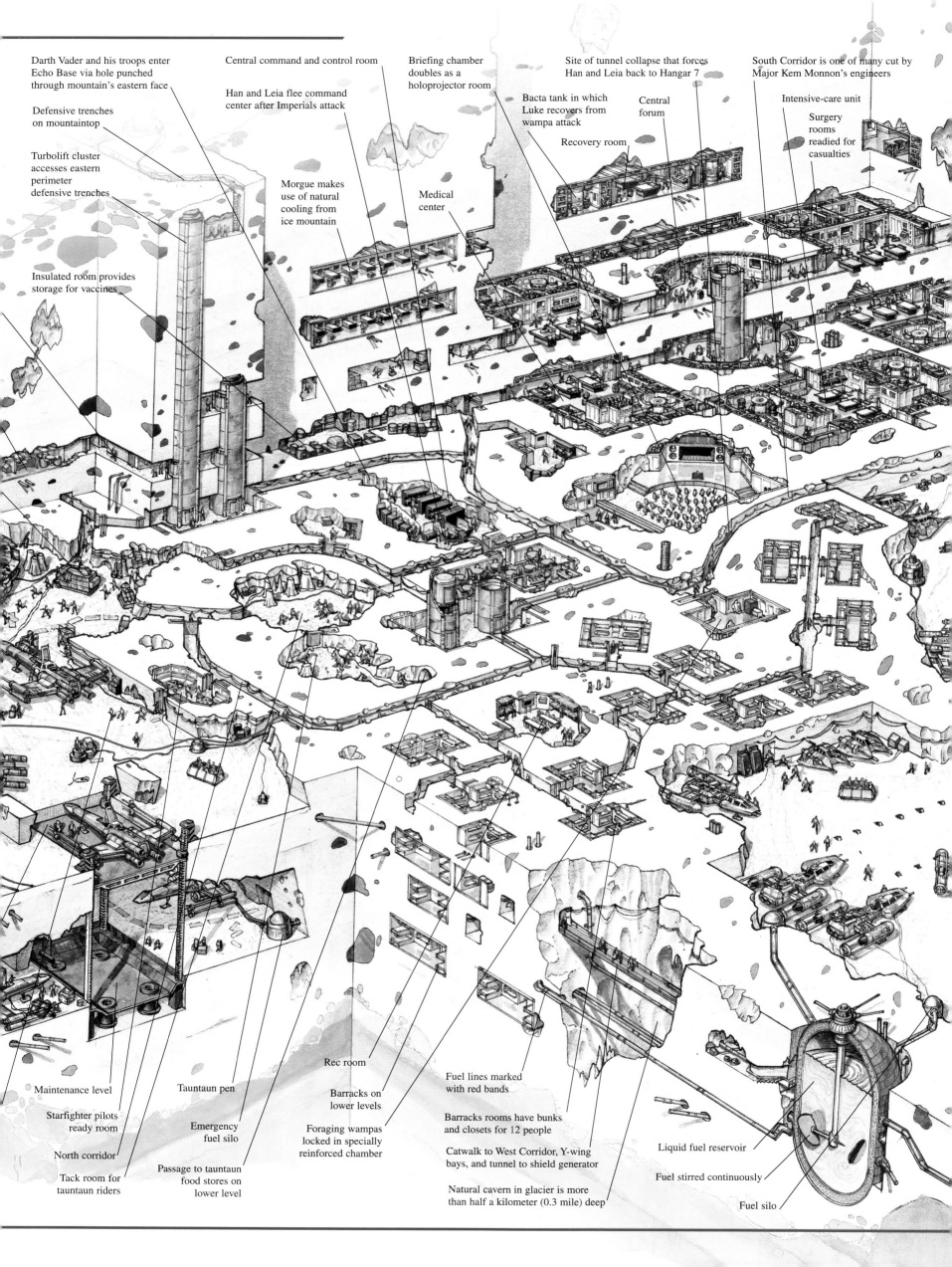

Darth Vader and his troops enter Echo Base via hole punched through mountain's eastern face

Defensive trenches on mountaintop

Turbolift cluster accesses eastern perimeter defensive trenches

Insulated room provides storage for vaccines

Central command and control room

Han and Leia flee command center after Imperials attack

Morgue makes use of natural cooling from ice mountain

Medical center

Briefing chamber doubles as a holoprojector room

Site of tunnel collapse that forces Han and Leia back to Hangar 7

Bacta tank in which Luke recovers from wampa attack

Recovery room

Central forum

South Corridor is one of many cut by Major Kem Monnon's engineers

Intensive-care unit

Surgery rooms readied for casualties

Maintenance level

Starfighter pilots ready room

North corridor

Tack room for tauntaun riders

Tauntaun pen

Emergency fuel silo

Passage to tauntaun food stores on lower level

Rec room

Barracks on lower levels

Foraging wampas locked in specially reinforced chamber

Fuel lines marked with red bands

Barracks rooms have bunks and closets for 12 people

Catwalk to West Corridor, Y-wing bays, and tunnel to shield generator

Natural cavern in glacier is more than half a kilometer (0.3 mile) deep

Liquid fuel reservoir

Fuel stirred continuously

Fuel silo

ECHO BASE

AFTER THE EVACUATION of Yavin 4, the Rebel Alliance embarked on a search for a planet or moon to serve as a new secret base of operations. Explorations by Luke Skywalker, Commander Narra, and others lead to the ice planet Hoth, a world so remote as to be off the standard navigational star charts entirely. The command center is constructed over the course of two standard years, under brutal conditions. Rebel engineers and construction crews employ laser ice-cutting equipment to enlarge a series of natural caverns, excavate new ones, and fashion connecting corridors. Designated Echo Base for the cave's strange acoustics, the base is still being constructed when an Imperial probe droid plunges fatefully to Hoth's glacial surface....

Snowspeeders and X-wings are stationed in North Hangar 7. Secret tunnels connect the hangar to several other, smaller north entrances.

PREPARING FOR THE WORST

While essential for defense, the presence of the shield generator all but guarantees that Echo Base will eventually unmask itself to the Empire. Anticipating that any assault would be launched on the surface of Hoth, General Carlist Rieekan orders that heavy blast doors be installed in the north and south entrances, trenches be excavated on the glacial plains all around the base, and that ground-based anti-personnel batteries be embedded in the mountainside above the principal hangars and in the ice fields between artillery trenches.

Laser ice-cutter is one of many that enlarged the mountain's caves

Leia's quarters

Door to Luke's quarters

Sunlight filters into base through narrow crevasse in the surface ice

Curved transparisteel window overlooks Hangar 7

Millennium Falcon's hyperdrive has yet to be fully repaired

Incom T-47 airspeeders modified to function on Hoth

Air boss oversees starfighter launch

R2-D2 searches for his counterpart

"Hobbie" Klivian and Kesin Ommis in Rogue 4 snowspeeder

Routing illuminators guide snowspeeders to launch area

Wedge Antilles and Wes Janson in Rogue 3 snowspeeder

Zev Senesca in Rogue 2 snowspeeder

Luke Skywalker and Dack Ralter in Rogue Leader

Major Dervis's infantry hurry to defensive trenches

Track for sliding door needs constant lubrication

North entrance blast door

Luke's X-wing will be transported to South entrance before last transport leaves

Hangar 7

Elevator to maintenance level

Snubfighter's astromech droid socket

Pilots and techs hurry to prepped crafts

EMERGENCY CARE

The Rebel Alliance is careful to provide timely medical support for its valued troops. On Hoth, a well-equipped medical center provides first-rate response and triage for Echo Base's 7,500 combat personnel. Overseen by a medical command officer, the staff of 350 physicians and surgeons, augmented by some 120 specialized droids, remains on call, to deal with any emergencies that might arise.

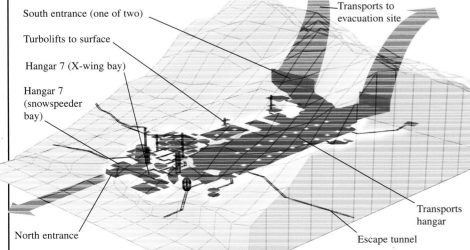

South entrance (one of two)

Turbolifts to surface

Hangar 7 (X-wing bay)

Hangar 7 (snowspeeder bay)

North entrance

Transports to evacuation site

Transports hangar

Escape tunnel

ICE MOUNTAIN HIDE-OUT

Several locations in Hoth's temperate zone were scouted and surveyed before a cavern-hollowed mountain in the southern Clabburn Range was judged suitable to serve as the hidden fortress the Rebels had in mind. The Corp of Engineers fashioned interior spaces vast enough to house not only the Alliance's wings of starfighters, but also its tattered fleet of Gallofree Yards transports. Plasmold insulation and armored doors—of a different sort than those used on Yavin 4—helped to shelter the base from the ferocity of Hoth's ice storms.

BATTLE OF HOTH

HOTH IS OFTEN CITED as the worst battlefield defeat suffered by the Rebel Alliance during the Galactic Civil War. It is Admiral Ozzel, however, who grants the Rebels time to mount a holding action—and the ensuing organized retreat—by arrogantly bringing the Imperial fleet out of hyperspace too close to Hoth. Darth Vader adds to the blunder by being so fixed on capturing Luke Skywalker alive that he orders his flotilla of Star Destroyers to pursue the *Falcon* rather than hunt down the escaped Rebel transports. Moreover, Civil War historians have pointed out that if not for this painful rout, the Alliance might never have risked everything at Endor a year later, where they inflicted a defeat on the Empire from which it never recovered.

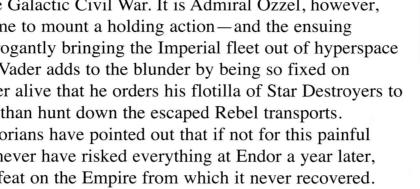

1 One of thousands seeded by the Imperial Star Destroyer *Stalker*, an Arakyd Viper probe droid meanders over Hoth's snowfields and glaciers, alert for anomalous energy signatures that might point to Rebel Alliance activity. Its images of the Rebel power generator are transmitted back to Imperial officers.

2 In the trenches, Beta Outpost troops commanded by Trey Callum ready their repeating blasters for in-close fighting. Precision targeting by anti-personnel batteries decimate Veers' snowtroopers, buying the Rebels more time to evacuate the base and weave their transports through the star destroyer blockade.

IMPERIAL GROUND ASSAULT

General Maximillian Veers is tasked with destroying the shield power generator and capturing rather than killing the Rebels who survive his assault. Forced to steer clear of the shield perimeter, Imperial landing barges and troop transports set down on the precarious Moorsh Moraine, well north of the heavily fortified mountain base. Having thus surrendered all element of surprise, but augmented with legions of snowtroopers, Veers' contingent of AT-ATs (large, four-legged walkers), AT-STs (medium bipeds), AT-ARs (faster, better armored bipeds), and AT-PTs (small, one-man scouts)—dubbed Blizzard Force—begins its inexorable march on the Rebel facility.

3 Swiveling on their bases, Golan Arms DF9 anti-artillery batteries hammer away at the advancing walkers, but to no avail. Snowspeeder pilots, too, find their lasers ineffective against the thick armor of the Imperial war machines. Raked by laserfire, Rogue Leader is hit, and Luke's gunner, Dack, is killed.

4 Following Luke's orders, Wedge and his gunner, Wes Janson, deploy Rogue 3's harpoon and tow cable against the AT-AT commanded by Brigadier General Nevar. The dangerous maneuver requires that the cable be wrapped around the legs of a walker, then severed at precisely the right moment.

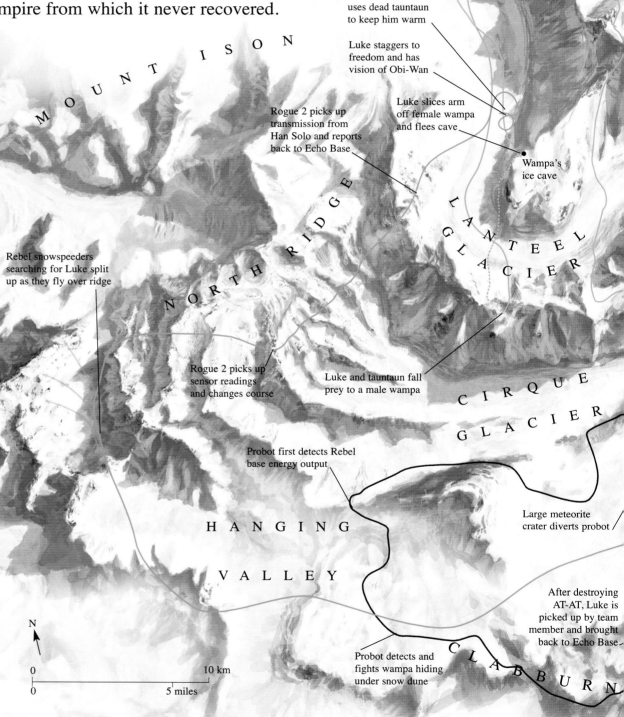

M O U N T I S O N

N O R T H   R I D G E

L A N T E E L   G L A C I E R

C I R Q U E   G L A C I E R

H A N G I N G   V A L L E Y

C L A B B U R N

Han finds Luke and uses dead tauntaun to keep him warm

Luke staggers to freedom and has vision of Obi-Wan

Luke slices arm off female wampa and flees cave

Rogue 2 picks up transmission from Han Solo and reports back to Echo Base

Wampa's ice cave

Rebel snowspeeders searching for Luke split up as they fly over ridge

Rogue 2 picks up sensor readings and changes course

Luke and tauntaun fall prey to a male wampa

Probot first detects Rebel base energy output

Large meteorite crater diverts probot

After destroying AT-AT, Luke is picked up by team member and brought back to Echo Base

Probot detects and fights wampa hiding under snow dune

N

0 ——— 10 km

0 ——— 5 miles

5 Its four legs ensnared by the high-tension tow cable, Blizzard 2 crashes to the unyielding tundra, leaving the rear of its neck vulnerable to follow-up laser fire. With one walker dispatched, the Rebels continue to wage their holding action, but are ultimately overwhelmed by the Empire's durable behemoths.

REBEL SHIELD SYSTEM

By dumping absorbed energy directly into the planet interior, the Rebels' planet-based shield withstands bombardments that would overwhelm ship shields. Only slow-moving ground-contact vehicles, like Imperial walkers, can traverse the outer surface. With the projector modules distributed throughout Rebel territory, Veers targets the central power generator.

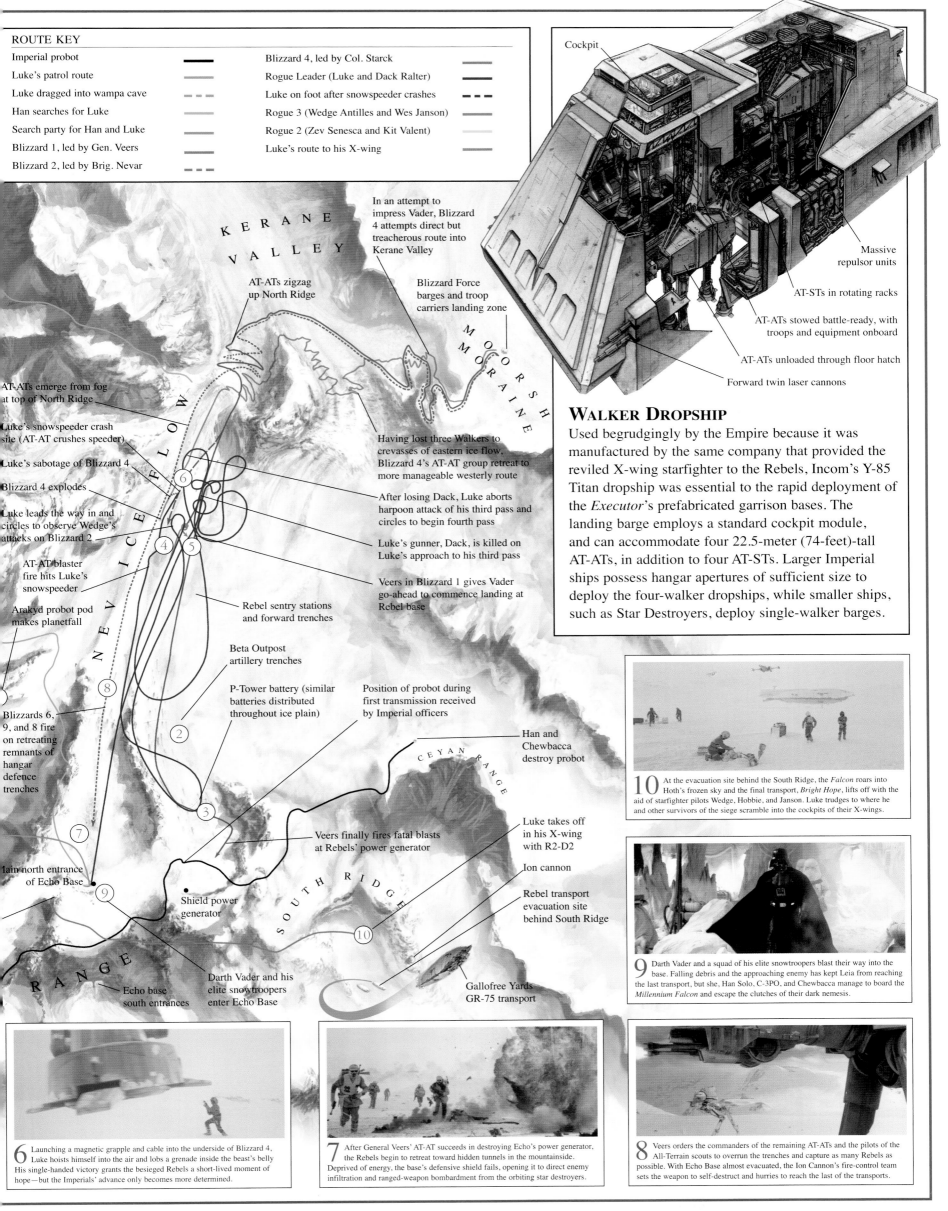

ROUTE KEY

Imperial probot

Luke's patrol route

Luke dragged into wampa cave

Han searches for Luke

Search party for Han and Luke

Blizzard 1, led by Gen. Veers

Blizzard 2, led by Brig. Nevar

Blizzard 4, led by Col. Starck

Rogue Leader (Luke and Dack Ralter)

Luke on foot after snowspeeder crashes

Rogue 3 (Wedge Antilles and Wes Janson)

Rogue 2 (Zev Senesca and Kit Valent)

Luke's route to his X-wing

KERANE VALLEY

In an attempt to impress Vader, Blizzard 4 attempts direct but treacherous route into Kerane Valley

AT-ATs zigzag up North Ridge

Blizzard Force barges and troop carriers landing zone

MOORSH MORAINE

AT-ATs emerge from fog at top of North Ridge

Luke's snowspeeder crash site (AT-AT crushes speeder)

Luke's sabotage of Blizzard 4

Blizzard 4 explodes

Luke leads the way in and circles to observe Wedge's attacks on Blizzard 2

AT-AT blaster fire hits Luke's snowspeeder

Arakyd probot pod makes planetfall

Blizzards 6, 9, and 8 fire on retreating remnants of hangar defence trenches

Main north entrance of Echo Base

NEVICE ICE FLOW

Having lost three Walkers to crevasses of eastern ice flow, Blizzard 4's AT-AT group retreat to more manageable westerly route

After losing Dack, Luke aborts harpoon attack of his third pass and circles to begin fourth pass

Luke's gunner, Dack, is killed on Luke's approach to his third pass

Veers in Blizzard 1 gives Vader go-ahead to commence landing at Rebel base

Rebel sentry stations and forward trenches

Beta Outpost artillery trenches

P-Tower battery (similar batteries distributed throughout ice plain)

Position of probot during first transmission received by Imperial officers

CEYAN RANGE

Han and Chewbacca destroy probot

Luke takes off in his X-wing with R2-D2

Ion cannon

Rebel transport evacuation site behind South Ridge

Veers finally fires fatal blasts at Rebels' power generator

SOUTH RIDGE

Shield power generator

RANGE

Echo base south entrances

Darth Vader and his elite snowtroopers enter Echo Base

Gallofree Yards GR-75 transport

WALKER DROPSHIP

Cockpit

Massive repulsor units

AT-STs in rotating racks

AT-ATs stowed battle-ready, with troops and equipment onboard

AT-ATs unloaded through floor hatch

Forward twin laser cannons

Used begrudgingly by the Empire because it was manufactured by the same company that provided the reviled X-wing starfighter to the Rebels, Incom's Y-85 Titan dropship was essential to the rapid deployment of the *Executor*'s prefabricated garrison bases. The landing barge employs a standard cockpit module, and can accommodate four 22.5-meter (74-feet)-tall AT-ATs, in addition to four AT-STs. Larger Imperial ships possess hangar apertures of sufficient size to deploy the four-walker dropships, while smaller ships, such as Star Destroyers, deploy single-walker barges.

10 At the evacuation site behind the South Ridge, the *Falcon* roars into Hoth's frozen sky and the final transport, *Bright Hope*, lifts off with the aid of starfighter pilots Wedge, Hobbie, and Janson. Luke trudges to where he and other survivors of the siege scramble into the cockpits of their X-wings.

9 Darth Vader and a squad of his elite snowtroopers blast their way into the base. Falling debris and the approaching enemy has kept Leia from reaching the last transport, but she, Han Solo, C-3PO, and Chewbacca manage to board the *Millennium Falcon* and escape the clutches of their dark nemesis.

6 Launching a magnetic grapple and cable into the underside of Blizzard 4, Luke hoists himself into the air and lobs a grenade inside the beast's belly. His single-handed victory grants the besieged Rebels a short-lived moment of hope—but the Imperials' advance only becomes more determined.

7 After General Veers' AT-AT succeeds in destroying Echo's power generator, the Rebels begin to retreat toward hidden tunnels in the mountainside. Deprived of energy, the base's defensive shield fails, opening it to direct enemy infiltration and ranged-weapon bombardment from the orbiting star destroyers.

8 Veers orders the commanders of the remaining AT-ATs and the pilots of the All-Terrain scouts to overrun the trenches and capture as many Rebels as possible. With Echo Base almost evacuated, the Ion Cannon's fire-control team sets the weapon to self-destruct and hurries to reach the last of the transports.

- South Entrance control room
- Transports and X-wing escorts move toward South Ridge evacuation launch site; 17 of the fleet of 30 are destroyed by Imperial blockade
- High-capacity personnel bus is surface-effect only
- Personnel evacuate Echo Base when word is received that a flotilla of Star Destroyers has emerged from hyperspace at the edge of the Hoth System
- Rebel soldiers on tauntaunback
- Flight crew shuttle
- Gallofree transport *Thon's Orchard*
- Cargo tug equipped with repulsorlift engine
- Ice column reinforced with plasteel rods
- Snowspeeders stashed wherever space allows
- Cargo modules bound for transports
- the base, *Bright Hope*, is loaded ded soldiers from the battlefield

ROUTE KEY

Han and Leia's escape route ——————

Ion Blasts

Synchronized with a battle-theater shield generator, the Kuat Drive Yard v-150 Ion Cannon fires massive, charged-plasma shots powerful enough to penetrate the ray shielding of an Imperial Star Destroyer in low orbit, neutralizing its weapons, shields, and engines—or, at the very least, disrupt control systems and ion drives. Drawbacks include a lengthy activation and targeting period, a low discharge rate of one volley per six seconds, and slow rotation as it aims.

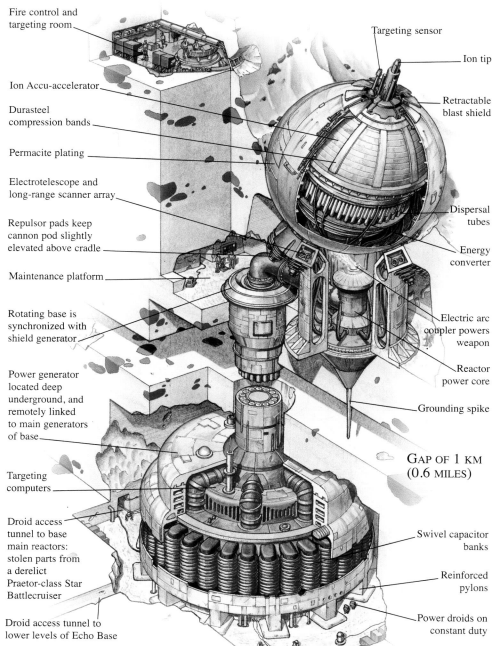

- Fire control and targeting room
- Targeting sensor
- Ion tip
- Retractable blast shield
- Ion Accu-accelerator
- Durasteel compression bands
- Permacite plating
- Electrotelescope and long-range scanner array
- Repulsor pads keep cannon pod slightly elevated above cradle
- Maintenance platform
- Rotating base is synchronized with shield generator
- Power generator located deep underground, and remotely linked to main generators of base
- Targeting computers
- Droid access tunnel to base main reactors: stolen parts from a derelict Praetor-class Star Battlecruiser
- Droid access tunnel to lower levels of Echo Base
- Dispersal tubes
- Energy converter
- Electric arc coupler powers weapon
- Reactor power core
- Grounding spike
- Swivel capacitor banks
- Reinforced pylons
- Power droids on constant duty

GAP OF 1 KM
(0.6 MILES)

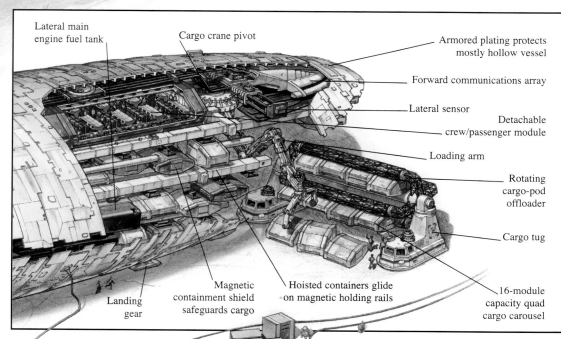

- Lateral main engine fuel tank
- Cargo crane pivot
- Armored plating protects mostly hollow vessel
- Forward communications array
- Lateral sensor
- Detachable crew/passenger module
- Loading arm
- Rotating cargo-pod offloader
- Cargo tug
- Landing gear
- Magnetic containment shield safeguards cargo
- Hoisted containers glide on magnetic holding rails
- 16-module capacity quad cargo carousel

Medium Transport

Little more than armored shells, 300-feet (90-meter)-long Gallofree Yards GR-75 transports are perfectly suited to the needs of the Rebel Alliance because of the relative ease of their loading and unloading process, their enormous cargo capacity, and their ability to land directly on the surface of a planet or moon. In transit, the GR-75's modular cargo pods are suspended from magnetic rails and kept in place by a powerful magnetic containment field. The ships were sold to the Alliance at a bargain, and used chiefly for transporting weapons, raw materials, food, fuel, and spare parts, though a few Gallofrees were retrofitted for personnel transport by adapting the interiors to accommodate sealed passenger pods.

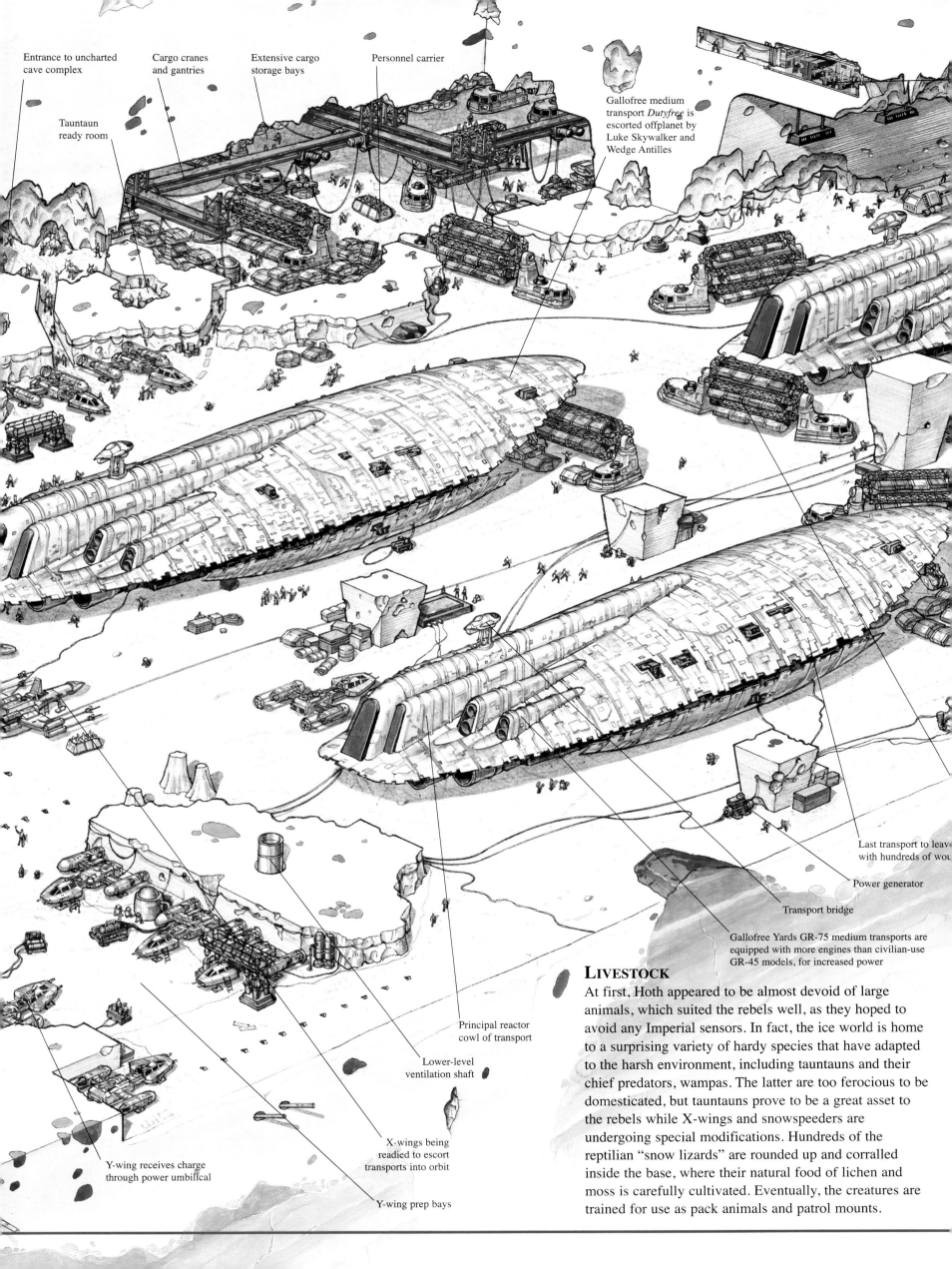

Entrance to uncharted cave complex

Cargo cranes and gantries

Extensive cargo storage bays

Personnel carrier

Tauntaun ready room

Gallofree medium transport *Dutyfree* is escorted offplanet by Luke Skywalker and Wedge Antilles

Last transport to leave with hundreds of wou

Power generator

Transport bridge

Gallofree Yards GR-75 medium transports are equipped with more engines than civilian-use GR-45 models, for increased power

Principal reactor cowl of transport

Lower-level ventilation shaft

X-wings being readied to escort transports into orbit

Y-wing receives charge through power umbilical

Y-wing prep bays

LIVESTOCK

At first, Hoth appeared to be almost devoid of large animals, which suited the rebels well, as they hoped to avoid any Imperial sensors. In fact, the ice world is home to a surprising variety of hardy species that have adapted to the harsh environment, including tauntauns and their chief predators, wampas. The latter are too ferocious to be domesticated, but tauntauns prove to be a great asset to the rebels while X-wings and snowspeeders are undergoing special modifications. Hundreds of the reptilian "snow lizards" are rounded up and corralled inside the base, where their natural food of lichen and moss is carefully cultivated. Eventually, the creatures are trained for use as pack animals and patrol mounts.

DAGOBAH

Near death from exposure to Hoth's sub-zero temperatures, the side of his face crushed by a giant wampa, Luke has a vision of his mentor, Obi-Wan Kenobi. The Jedi Master orders him to go to the Dagobah system to complete his training under the guidance of Kenobi's former instructor, the diminutive Yoda. With a bewildered R2-D2 for companionship, Luke parts with Han and Leia to follow his destined course. Remote from known space routes, shrouded in cloud cover but emitting massive life-form readings, Dagobah is a gloomy world of swamps and twisted trees, winged predators and poisonous snakes. Seemingly engulfed by the planet, Luke's X-wing plummets to the surface....

1 "Is this a dream or just a bad idea?" Luke wonders aloud. His mind as foggy as his new environment, he leaves his crashed starfighter to marinate in the muck of one of Dagobah's black-water bogs and begins to take stock of the inhospitable world to which Obi-Wan has sent him.

2 While Luke can't help feeling that there is something strangely recognizable about haunted Dagobah, there is nothing even remotely familiar about the gnomish green creature who shows up to turn Luke and R2-D2's camp into his private playground.

3 In the creature's cramped dwelling, while torrential rain falls, Luke learns that he has in fact found Yoda. But the ancient Jedi Master and a ghostly Obi-Wan Kenobi disagree about whether Luke will be able to surrender his yearning for adventure and be properly trained in the ways of the Force.

4 Under Yoda's sometimes mystifying tutelage, Luke learns to perform superhuman tasks and will his body to levitate objects—including the astromech. With Yoda clasped to his back, Luke runs, leaps, and somersaults through Dagobah's riotous jungle, his strength flowing from the Force.

5 Deep within the cave-like root system of a colossal gnarltree—a domain of thick-bodied snakes and quick-tongued sleens—Luke has a precognitive vision of the true relationship with his evil adversary, Darth Vader. Strong with the dark side, the cave contains no more than what Luke has taken with him.

Yoda gathers galla seeds and sohli bark from areas surrounding his home

Spring-fed sweet water lagoon

Gnarltree bridge over lagoon inlet

Yoda's house

R2-D2 peers through the window of Yoda's dwelling

Yoda often gathers yarum seeds from forest, avoiding the sharp webs spun by butcherbugs

Parasitic blackvine forms natural bridges

6 Yoda demonstrates to Luke that "size matters not," when he telekinetically rescues Luke's sinking X-wing from the grasp of the sticky bog. Disappointed with Luke, Yoda explains that the youth's failed attempt was due to his inability to believe in his own potential and the power of the Force.

7 A vision of Han and Leia imperiled on a city in the clouds persuades Luke to abbreviate his training and leave Dagobah—despite Yoda's admonition that, by doing so, Luke will likely destroy all for which Han and Leia have fought and suffered.

DISMAL AND DANGEROUS

Dagobah's bogs and lagoons are home to a host of creatures, including the swamp slug, which pulverizes its prey between thousands of tiny grinding teeth; the stealthy dragonsnake, whose razor-sharp claws are strong enough to incise alloy; and the quick-striking scrange, which uses its tusked tail to make short work of any creature that wanders into its reach. Smaller, but equally deadly, is the butcherbug, which spins slicing webs, and the morp, whose venom causes paralysis.

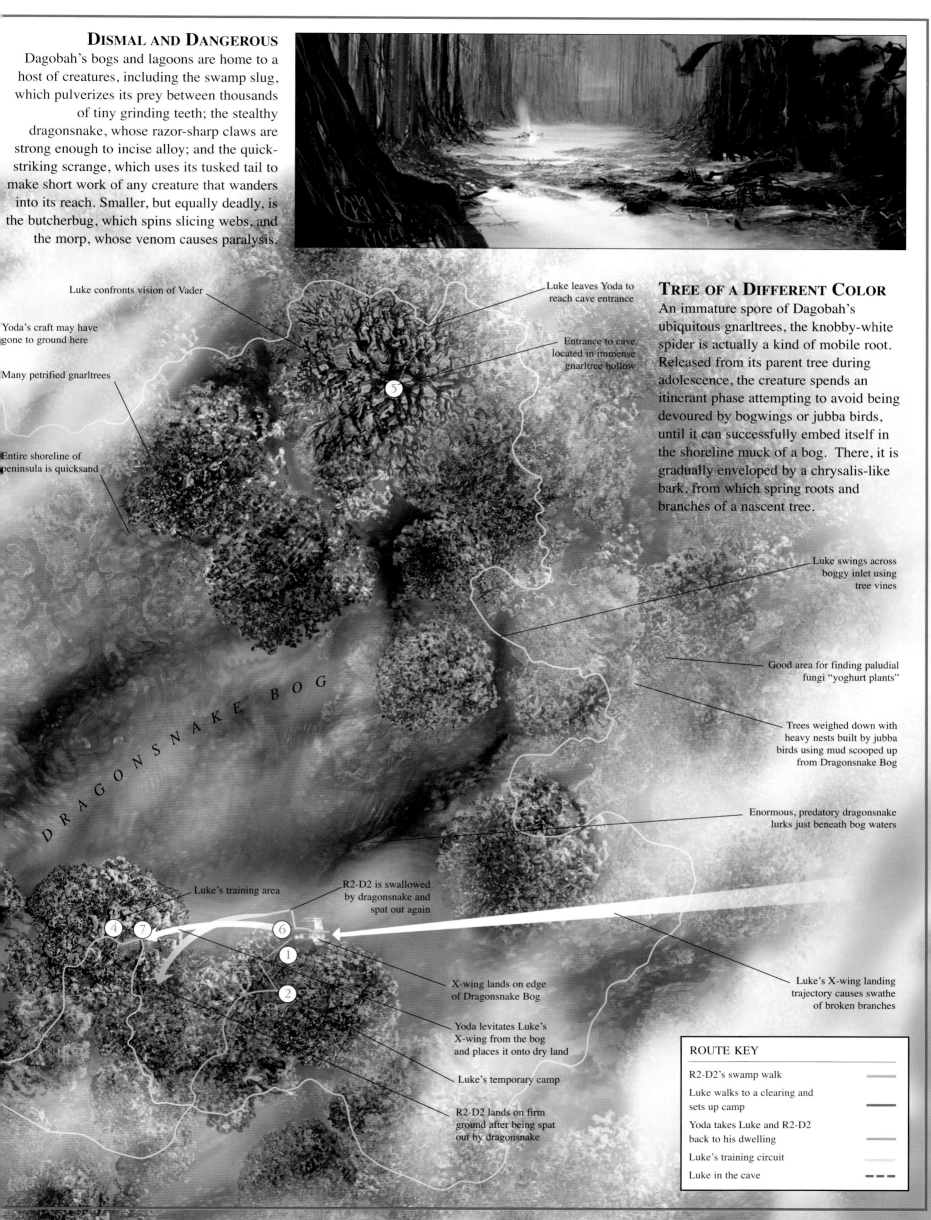

Luke confronts vision of Vader

Yoda's craft may have gone to ground here

Many petrified gnarltrees

Entire shoreline of peninsula is quicksand

Luke leaves Yoda to reach cave entrance

Entrance to cave located in immense gnarltree hollow

TREE OF A DIFFERENT COLOR

An immature spore of Dagobah's ubiquitous gnarltrees, the knobby-white spider is actually a kind of mobile root. Released from its parent tree during adolescence, the creature spends an itinerant phase attempting to avoid being devoured by bogwings or jubba birds, until it can successfully embed itself in the shoreline muck of a bog. There, it is gradually enveloped by a chrysalis-like bark, from which spring roots and branches of a nascent tree.

Luke swings across boggy inlet using tree vines

Good area for finding paludial fungi "yoghurt plants"

Trees weighed down with heavy nests built by jubba birds using mud scooped up from Dragonsnake Bog

DRAGONSNAKE BOG

Enormous, predatory dragonsnake lurks just beneath bog waters

Luke's training area

R2-D2 is swallowed by dragonsnake and spat out again

Luke's X-wing landing trajectory causes swathe of broken branches

X-wing lands on edge of Dragonsnake Bog

Yoda levitates Luke's X-wing from the bog and places it onto dry land

Luke's temporary camp

R2-D2 lands on firm ground after being spat out by dragonsnake

ROUTE KEY

R2-D2's swamp walk	——
Luke walks to a clearing and sets up camp	——
Yoda takes Luke and R2-D2 back to his dwelling	——
Luke's training circuit	——
Luke in the cave	- - -

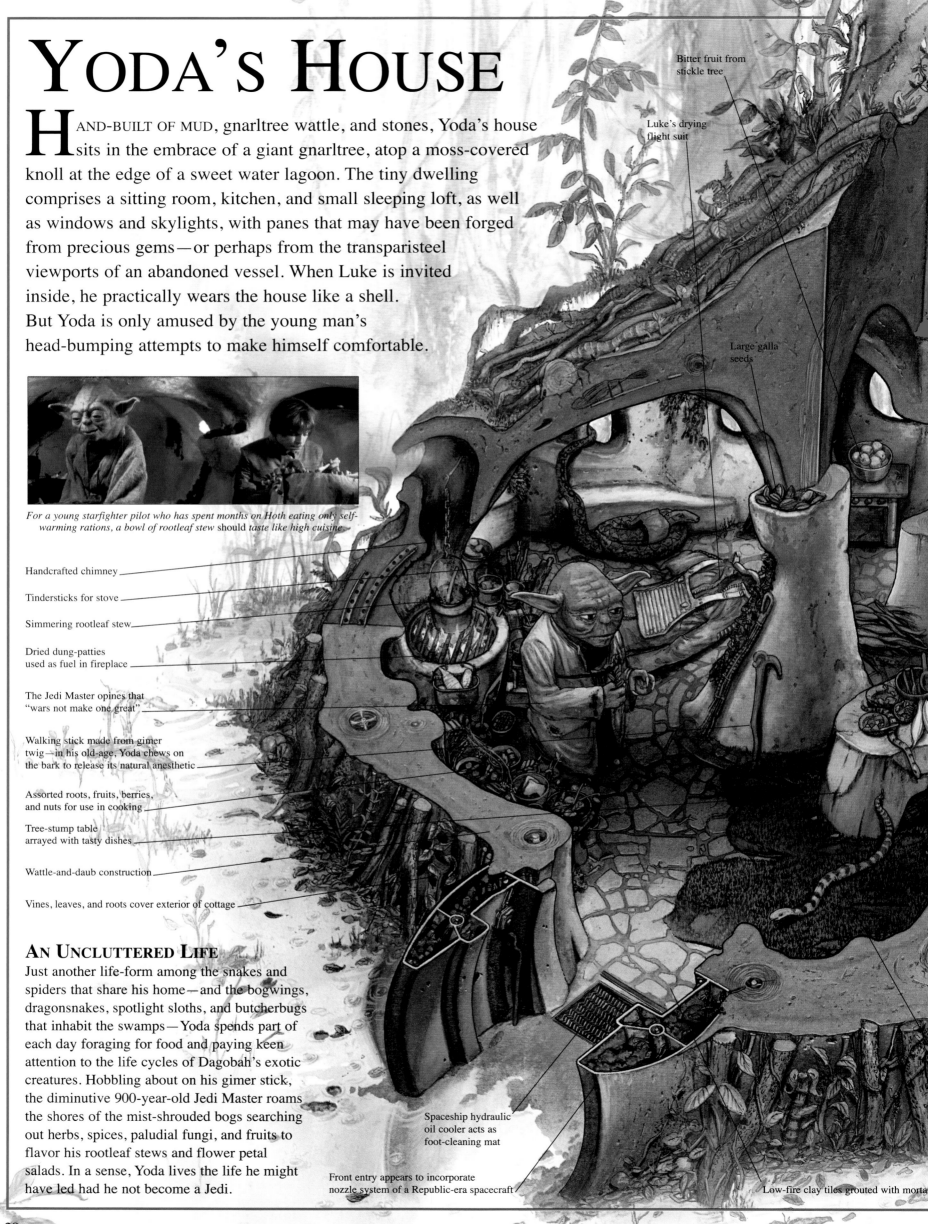

YODA'S HOUSE

HAND-BUILT OF MUD, gnarltree wattle, and stones, Yoda's house sits in the embrace of a giant gnarltree, atop a moss-covered knoll at the edge of a sweet water lagoon. The tiny dwelling comprises a sitting room, kitchen, and small sleeping loft, as well as windows and skylights, with panes that may have been forged from precious gems—or perhaps from the transparisteel viewports of an abandoned vessel. When Luke is invited inside, he practically wears the house like a shell. But Yoda is only amused by the young man's head-bumping attempts to make himself comfortable.

For a young starfighter pilot who has spent months on Hoth eating only self-warming rations, a bowl of rootleaf stew should taste like high cuisine.

Bitter fruit from stickle tree

Luke's drying flight suit

Large galla seeds

Handcrafted chimney

Tindersticks for stove

Simmering rootleaf stew

Dried dung-patties used as fuel in fireplace

The Jedi Master opines that "wars not make one great"

Walking stick made from gimer twig—in his old-age, Yoda chews on the bark to release its natural anesthetic

Assorted roots, fruits, berries, and nuts for use in cooking

Tree-stump table arrayed with tasty dishes

Wattle-and-daub construction

Vines, leaves, and roots cover exterior of cottage

AN UNCLUTTERED LIFE

Just another life-form among the snakes and spiders that share his home—and the bogwings, dragonsnakes, spotlight sloths, and butcherbugs that inhabit the swamps—Yoda spends part of each day foraging for food and paying keen attention to the life cycles of Dagobah's exotic creatures. Hobbling about on his gimer stick, the diminutive 900-year-old Jedi Master roams the shores of the mist-shrouded bogs searching out herbs, spices, paludial fungi, and fruits to flavor his rootleaf stews and flower petal salads. In a sense, Yoda lives the life he might have led had he not become a Jedi.

Spaceship hydraulic oil cooler acts as foot-cleaning mat

Front entry appears to incorporate nozzle system of a Republic-era spacecraft

Low-fire clay tiles grouted with mortar

Sleeping loft has woven mat and blanket

Rolled-up rope ladder

Luke's power lamp that Yoda claimed for himself

Makeshift nightlight made of projector elements from spaceship's artificial-gravity compensators

Sink fed by water drawn from sluice

Drying herbs (aid sleep)

Swamp squash

Luminous stone used for glowlamp

Backstrap-loomed cloth

A SECRET PURPOSE

Yoda knew of Dagobah long before he chose it to be his place of self-exile. While it might appear that in so doing he sentenced himself to a life of seclusion, self-denial, and hardship, or that he was seeking only to place himself far from the Emperor's reach, he had a deeper motive in mind. Absent distractions, or any means of leaving Dagobah to confront the Emperor or Darth Vader on his own, Yoda has been able to devote much of the last 22 standard years to deciphering ancient texts, meditating on particular aspects of the Force, and using his Jedi skills not only to communicate with Obi-Wan Kenobi, but also to monitor the maturation of the Skywalker twins. In fact, he is patiently awaiting the day they might help topple the Sith and return balance to the Force.

Tools, machete, spade, and digging spikes for uncovering edible roots

Box holds keepsakes, ancient texts, and Yoda's lightsaber

Growth rings in the oldest gnarltree roots that act as cottage frame

A fretful R2-D2 peeps inside dwelling

Spacecraft deck-plating forms sturdy, waterproof foundation to house

Rug made of spot-light sloth fur

Non-venomous vine snakes share space with Yoda

Local twigs and grasses reinforce plaster

Luke not sure just what he has gotten himself into

Burrows made by silver-nape beetles

Mud mixed with tree resin to complete water proofing of walls and floors

BEGUILING ENVIRONMENT

The Force was strong on Dagobah even before Yoda arrived. While he could have drawn on the Force to raise a home as elegant as the Jedi Temple on Coruscant, he instead fabricated a primitive abode that makes Obi-Wan's house on Tatooine seem palatial by comparison. Yoda's hut looks as if it could be reduced to rubble by one of Dagobah's torrential rainstorms, and in fact it did fall into ruin soon after his death. In the same way that Yoda uses the Force and the planet's natural defenses to discourage visitors from investigating Dagobah, he may also draw on the power inherent in Dagobah to hold the hut together.

CLOUD CITY

OUNDED BY ECCENTRIC INDUSTRIALIST Lord Ecclessis Figg of Corellia, Cloud City was originally known as Floating Home Mining Colony. Hovering at some 59,000 kilometers (37,000 miles) from Bespin's core, the installation is designed to extract rare tibanna gas from the lower atmosphere of the planet, which is then processed and packaged for shipment offworld. Now administered by former gambler Lando Calrissian, Cloud City has become an exclusive resort, drawing a select clientele of exceptionally wealthy tourists who stay in stylish, sway-flexible hotel-casinos—the Yerith Bespin and Pair O'Dice, among others—and enjoy Bespin's fabled two-hour-long sunsets.

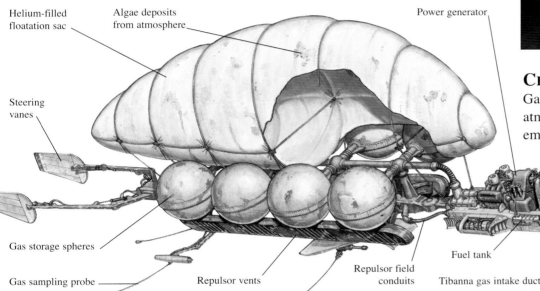

Helium-filled floatation sac

Algae deposits from atmosphere

Power generator

Steering vanes

Gas storage spheres

Gas sampling probe

Repulsor vents

Repulsor field conduits

Fuel tank

Tibanna gas intake duct

CHASING GAS STORMS

Gas prospectors have navigated Bespin's breathable upper atmosphere for many generations, and Cloud City still employs a legion of these freelance dare-devils to pinpoint lush pockets of spin-sealed Tibanna. Piloting their own jury-rigged craft through the clouds, prospectors seek to locate and exploit fresh eruptions of tibanna gas before the major contractors. Gas storms on Bespin are highly volatile and unpredictable, and, though the prospectors accept the risks for the sake of the sizeable profits, some pursuits are decidedly deadly.

FLOATING PARTNERSHIPS

Cloud City shares Bespin's extraordinary skies with smaller refineries. Kept aloft by massive repulsorlift generators, these mobile, automated facilities can re-orient themselves to draw tibanna from newly discovered pockets of gas. In general, however, these refineries handle surpluses from larger installations like Cloud City.

FRESH AIR

Constructed from materials mined from the Bespin System's innermost planet, Miser, Cloud City rises atop the 16-kilometer (10-mile)-wide mining structure. Its five million residents and visitors inhabit the planet's breathable upper atmosphere, known as the "Life Zone," which is replenished and shielded from the noxious lower atmosphere by a layer of airborne algae.

WATCH THE SKIES

With mining operations and tourism running unabated throughout Bespin's long year, the need for security is great. Stringent visa procedures are in place, and unidentified vessels are detected and intercepted long before they reach any of the docking platforms. A shield generator protects Cloud City from near-space bombardment and/or laser fire, but routine vigilance is overseen by the Wing Guard, which uses twin-pod cloud cars for patrol and emergency actions. The two-person fliers are outfitted with blaster cannons and can sustain an average speed of 1,500 kilometers per hour (930 mph). Employing both repulsorlifts and ion engines, the atmospheric airspeeders are also used as pleasure craft.

NOSTALGIC DECOR

Princess Leia's chamber is typical of the resort's luxury housing. The white, synthstone architecture is an homage to the style of the planet Alderaan, in honor of Lord Figg's wife, and coincidentally appropriate for the ex-diplomat. The elegant decor may also help soothe the nerves of the wealthy guests who gamble in the casinos and jostle for position in clubs and restaurants.

CARBONITE STORAGE REPULSOR SLED

Bespin Motors' carbonite sled is intended for use in conjunction with a carbon-freeze chamber for the safe transport of exotic gases that exist at high-pressure, such as tibanna. Tibanna is used in starcraft weaponry, hyperdrives, and as a coolant around the gravito-active elements of repulsorlifts. Inside the sled's control frame, a quantity of gas is suspended within a super-strong block of carbonite. Lord Vader decides to use Han Solo as a test subject for the storage of a humanoid within carbonite. By this process, Vader hopes to immobilize his son, Luke Skywalker, for transport to the Emperor. As he is lowered into the freezing chamber, Han is injected to induce hibernation before carbonite infuses and solidifies throughout his body.

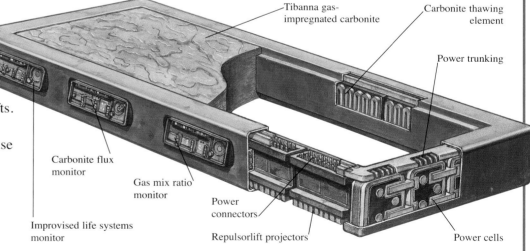

Tibanna gas-impregnated carbonite

Carbonite thawing element

Power trunking

Carbonite flux monitor

Gas mix ratio monitor

Power connectors

Repulsorlift projectors

Power cells

Improvised life systems monitor

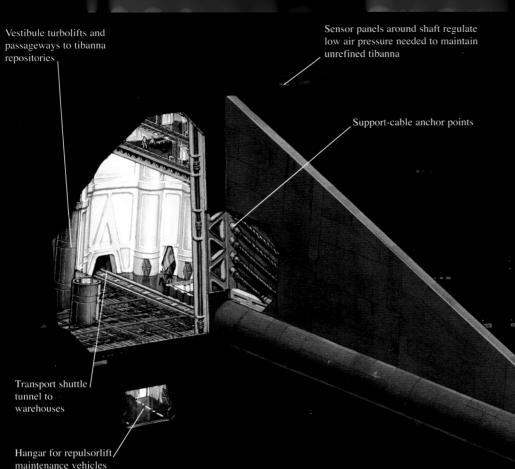

Vestibule turbolifts and passageways to tibanna repositories

Sensor panels around shaft regulate low air pressure needed to maintain unrefined tibanna

Support-cable anchor points

Transport shuttle tunnel to warehouses

Hangar for repulsorlift maintenance vehicles

Narrow transportation tunnel connects processing vane to rest of facility

Single-track conveyor alternately transports empty carbon-block frames into vane and filled blocks out

High-tensile support cables

HARD-PRESSED WORKERS

The monotonous and sometimes dangerous work of mining and processing tibanna gas is performed by Ugnaughts—porcine humanoids native to the planet Gentes—who reside in the floating metropolis's labyrinth of humid, red-lighted work corridors.

PROCESSING VANE

DEEP INSIDE THE BELLY of Cloud City, Darth Vader takes advantage of one of the airborne facility's gigantic gas-processing vanes for his own evil ends. He makes sinister use of a carbon-freeze chamber—where tibanna gas is admixed with carbonite for flash-freeze preservation—by having Han Solo encased in carbonite and placed in the custody of bounty hunter Boba Fett. The dark lord then battles Luke Skywalker onto a sensor balcony suspended over a vast reactor shaft, in which tibanna is stored at high pressure before purification and stabilization. Luke is finally sucked out of the shaft through a network of gas-exhaust pipes and ends up dangling from the underbelly of Cloud City, desperately clutching a weather vane.

Processing vane (area enlarged, *right*) situated on side of reactor shaft

Gas exhaust port into which Luke is sucked

City level

Tibanna block warehouse and conveyors

Transport docking bays

Tractor beam arrays line underbelly of pod

Ring of repulsorlifts holds city aloft

Weather/climate sensor vane

Heavily shielded main power converter and distribution node

Tibanna gas shoots up reactor stalk and is ducted into reactor shafts at top for processing

Power conduits and converters line side of stalk

Ring of ducts around reactor bulb allow mined gases to enter reactor stalk from aperture in underside of bulb

③

②

①

SPIN-SEALED RICHES

Generators located along Cloud City's underbelly emit tractor beams that converge below the reactor bulb to create an energy funnel. This funnel mines tibanna from Bespin's lower atmosphere at depths of more than 23,000 kilometers (14,200 miles). The gas passes via an aperture in the underside of the reactor bulb (1) to the reactor stalk (2) and into smaller reactor shafts (3), where it filters into processing vanes. The manufactured gas outperforms the energy produced by competing gases in starcraft weaponry and hyperdrives.

Only just managing to keep ahold of the teetering sensor balcony in the reactor shaft, Luke refuses to accept Vader's offer of an alliance—or his revelation that he is in fact Luke's father.

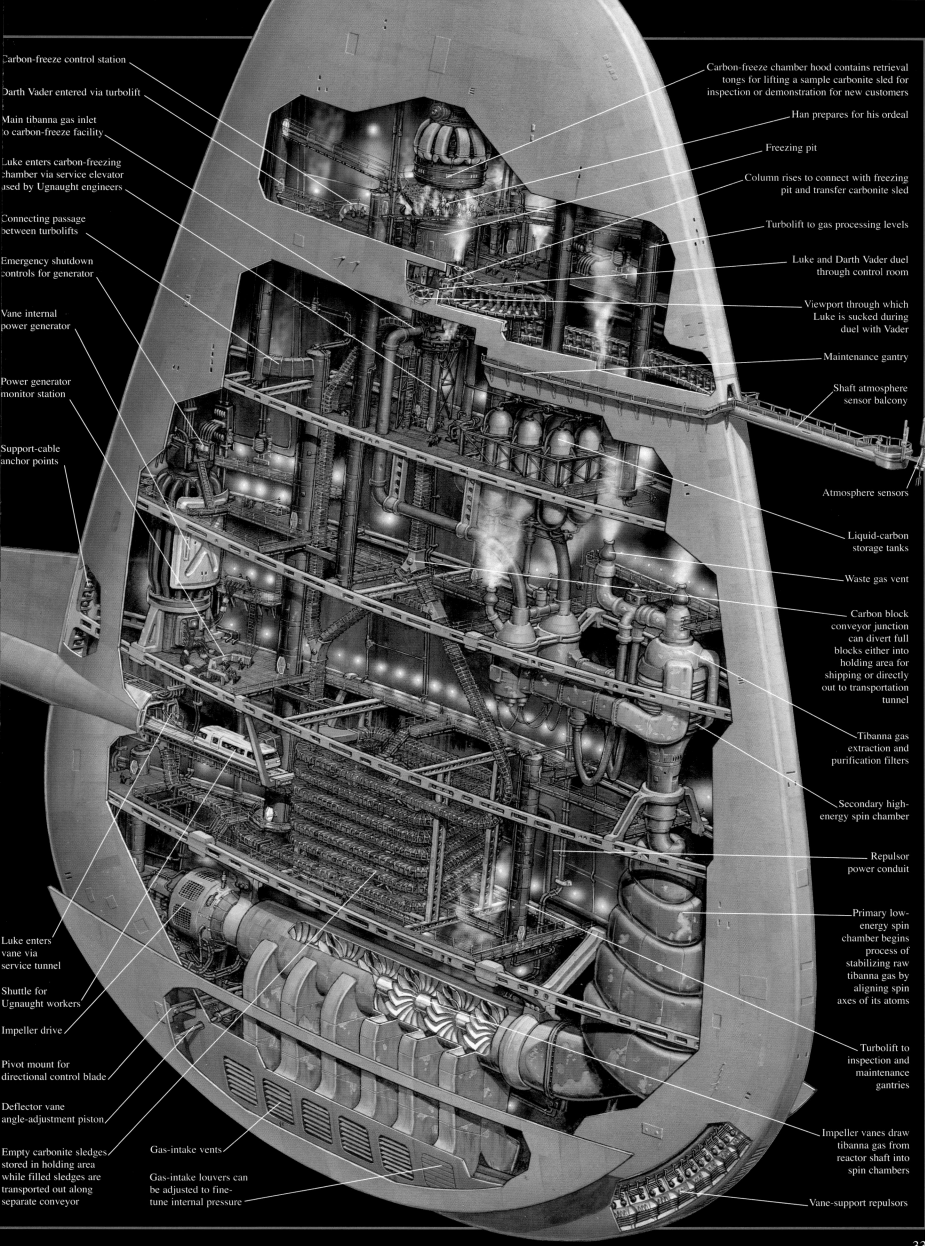

Carbon-freeze control station

Darth Vader entered via turbolift

Main tibanna gas inlet to carbon-freeze facility

Luke enters carbon-freezing chamber via service elevator used by Ugnaught engineers

Connecting passage between turbolifts

Emergency shutdown controls for generator

Vane internal power generator

Power generator monitor station

Support-cable anchor points

Luke enters vane via service tunnel

Shuttle for Ugnaught workers

Impeller drive

Pivot mount for directional control blade

Deflector vane angle-adjustment piston

Empty carbonite sledges stored in holding area while filled sledges are transported out along separate conveyor

Gas-intake vents

Gas-intake louvers can be adjusted to fine-tune internal pressure

Carbon-freeze chamber hood contains retrieval tongs for lifting a sample carbonite sled for inspection or demonstration for new customers

Han prepares for his ordeal

Freezing pit

Column rises to connect with freezing pit and transfer carbonite sled

Turbolift to gas processing levels

Luke and Darth Vader duel through control room

Viewport through which Luke is sucked during duel with Vader

Maintenance gantry

Shaft atmosphere sensor balcony

Atmosphere sensors

Liquid-carbon storage tanks

Waste gas vent

Carbon block conveyor junction can divert full blocks either into holding area for shipping or directly out to transportation tunnel

Tibanna gas extraction and purification filters

Secondary high-energy spin chamber

Repulsor power conduit

Primary low-energy spin chamber begins process of stabilizing raw tibanna gas by aligning spin axes of its atoms

Turbolift to inspection and maintenance gantries

Impeller vanes draw tibanna gas from reactor shaft into spin chambers

Vane-support repulsors

33

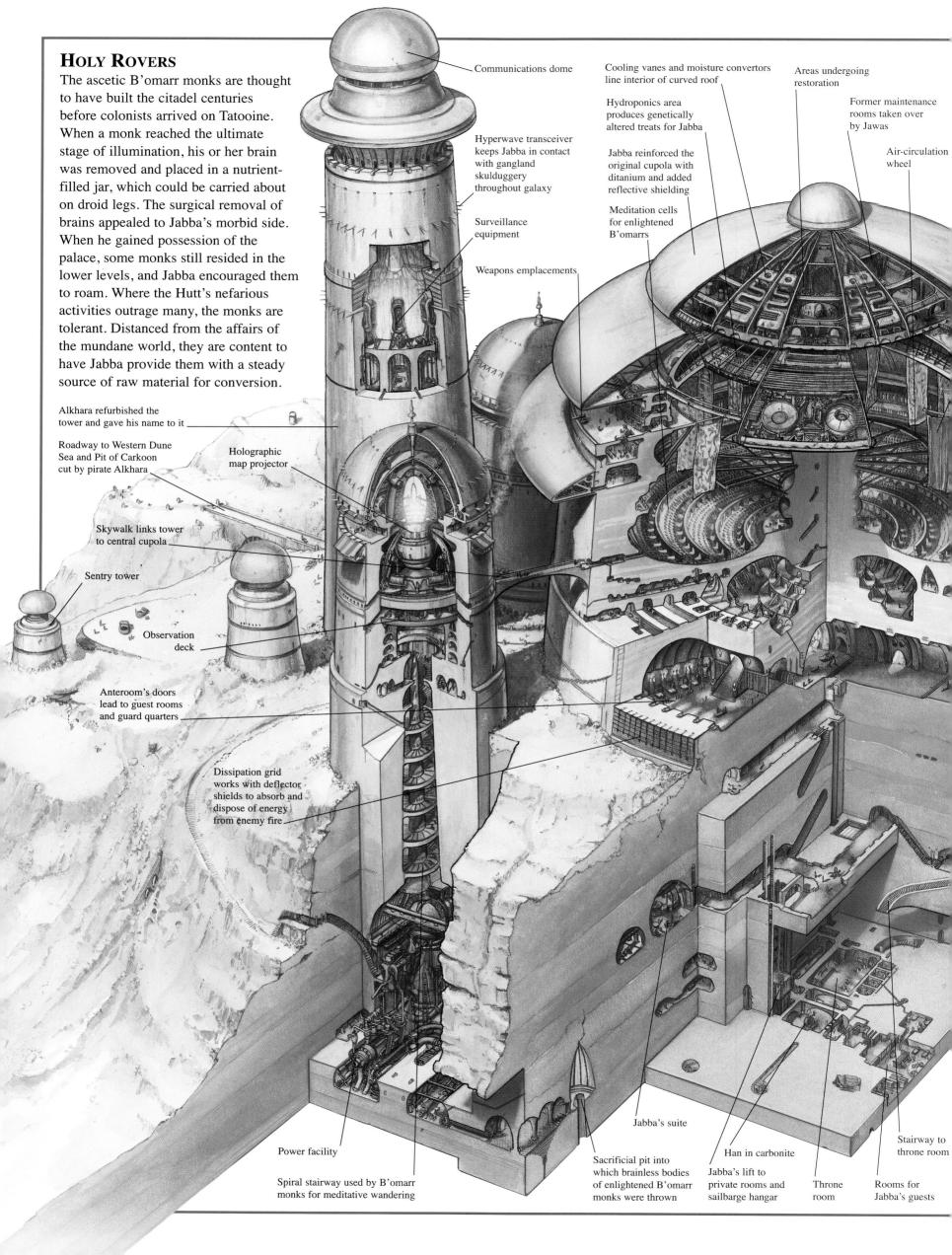

HOLY ROVERS

The ascetic B'omarr monks are thought to have built the citadel centuries before colonists arrived on Tatooine. When a monk reached the ultimate stage of illumination, his or her brain was removed and placed in a nutrient-filled jar, which could be carried about on droid legs. The surgical removal of brains appealed to Jabba's morbid side. When he gained possession of the palace, some monks still resided in the lower levels, and Jabba encouraged them to roam. Where the Hutt's nefarious activities outrage many, the monks are tolerant. Distanced from the affairs of the mundane world, they are content to have Jabba provide them with a steady source of raw material for conversion.

Communications dome

Hyperwave transceiver keeps Jabba in contact with gangland skulduggery throughout galaxy

Surveillance equipment

Cooling vanes and moisture convertors line interior of curved roof

Hydroponics area produces genetically altered treats for Jabba

Jabba reinforced the original cupola with ditanium and added reflective shielding

Meditation cells for enlightened B'omarrs

Weapons emplacements

Areas undergoing restoration

Former maintenance rooms taken over by Jawas

Air-circulation wheel

Alkhara refurbished the tower and gave his name to it

Roadway to Western Dune Sea and Pit of Carkoon cut by pirate Alkhara

Holographic map projector

Skywalk links tower to central cupola

Sentry tower

Observation deck

Anteroom's doors lead to guest rooms and guard quarters

Dissipation grid works with deflector shields to absorb and dispose of energy from enemy fire

Power facility

Spiral stairway used by B'omarr monks for meditative wandering

Sacrificial pit into which brainless bodies of enlightened B'omarr monks were thrown

Jabba's suite

Han in carbonite

Jabba's lift to private rooms and sailbarge hangar

Throne room

Stairway to throne room

Rooms for Jabba's guests

THIEVES AND MURDERERS

The bandit Alkhara was the first outsider to appropriate the B'omarr monastery for his own use. Among his legendary misdeeds, Alkhara had the members of a local police garrison murdered; then, in turn, he slaughtered the Sand People who had carried out the crime, thus initiating a blood feud between Tusken Raiders and settlers that exists to this day. Alkhara remained at the citadel for 34 years, before being driven off Tatooine by Jabba the Hutt.

SAIL BARGE HANGAR

Jabba is ferried across Tatooine in signature sail barges and skiffs designed by the Ubrikkian Corporation, but commissioned by architect Derren Flet. When it came to designing dungeons for the palace, however, Flet didn't fare nearly as well—he was executed for failing to take into account the number of beings Jabba would imprison, or the full extent of the Hutt's depravity.

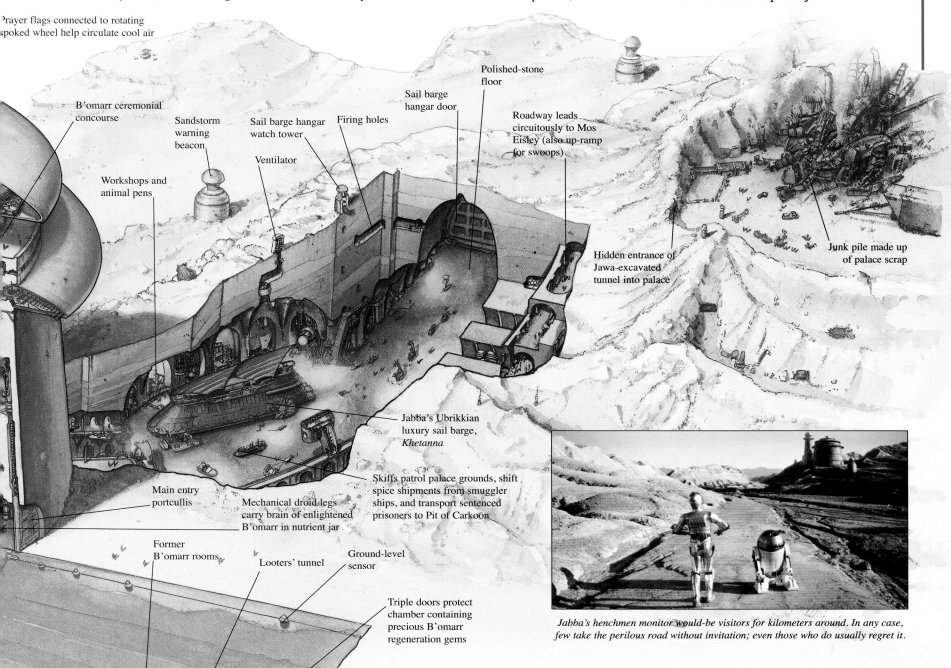

Prayer flags connected to rotating spoked wheel help circulate cool air

B'omarr ceremonial concourse

Sandstorm warning beacon

Workshops and animal pens

Sail barge hangar watch tower

Ventilator

Firing holes

Sail barge hangar door

Polished-stone floor

Roadway leads circuitously to Mos Eisley (also up-ramp for swoops)

Hidden entrance of Jawa-excavated tunnel into palace

Junk pile made up of palace scrap

Jabba's Ubrikkian luxury sail barge, *Khetanna*

Skiffs patrol palace grounds, shift spice shipments from smuggler ships, and transport sentenced prisoners to Pit of Carkoon

Main entry portcullis

Mechanical droid legs carry brain of enlightened B'omarr in nutrient jar

Former B'omarr rooms

Looters' tunnel

Ground-level sensor

Triple doors protect chamber containing precious B'omarr regeneration gems

High-quality spice cultivated underground

Earliest portion of monastery complex

B'omarr lecture hall was once adorned with tapestries and frescoes

Stairway to long-abandoned B'omarr mine

Jabba's henchmen monitor would-be visitors for kilometers around. In any case, few take the perilous road without invitation; even those who do usually regret it.

JABBA'S PALACE

VISIBLE FROM LOW ORBIT, the imposing citadel known as Jabba the Hutt's palace is so sprawling and well suited to its ruthless surroundings that it has become the most prominent feature of Tatooine's Northern Dune Sea. While inhabited by its original builders, the inscrutable order of B'omarr monks, the citadel was a place of forbidding seclusion. Then, for a time, it became the property of a fearless bandit and rogue, Alkhara, who added the nine-story tower, the battlements, and the dungeons. When the Hutt crime lord, Jabba, moved his base of operations to the lawless planet of Tatooine, he seized control of the citadel, taking over the cool, damp lower levels and reinforcing the exterior against enemy air strikes. Jabba now endows the palace with an atmosphere of unprecedented depravity and corruption.

JABBA'S THRONE ROOM

JABBA THE HUTT'S FONDNESS FOR murky underground places and theatricality leads him to convert a portion of the former B'omarr monastery into a presence, or throne, room, which he fills with his corrupt associates, cut-throat recruits, and sycophantic followers. At his command, the strains of jizz waft through the spicy air; dancers of exotic species gyrate across the stone floor; smugglers or weapons merchants who cross him are humiliated and thrown to the ferocious rancor beast — or a bounty hunter and his prisoner are admitted for audience.

THE BAND PLAYS ON

Made up of noted jizz wailers — some with prices on their head — the Max Rebo Band perform exclusively for Jabba, either at his palace or at his townhouse in Mos Eisley. The original band consisted of Max, Droopy McCool, and Sy Snootles, who played together in Evar Orbus and His Galactic Jizz-Wailers. The trio was forced to take matters in its own hands after Orbus's career was cut short — by a stray blaster bolt.

CORRUPT COURT

Only the most notorious smugglers and bounty hunters are allowed to consort openly in the throne room — those who have proved themselves adept at murder, mayhem, or crimes of high standing. Those of junior reputation roam the vast palace, forced to make do with entertaining Jabba's subordinates, and are afforded less respect than Jabba's chief droids. It is into this command, the intimidating atmosphere that Princess Leia, disguised as bounty hunter Boushh, enters.

From atop a colossal dais, Jabba the Hutt controls nearly everything in the throne room — including a trap door that leads to a rancor pit 7.5 meters (25 feet) below.

Singer Joh Yowza

Bith horn player Barquin D'an, brother of the illustrious Figrin D'an

Rodian slitherhorn player Doda Bodonawieedo

Lando Calrissian, disguised as skiff guard Tamtel Skreej

Dancer Yarna d'al' Gargan

Band leader Max Rebo

Jabba's Kowakian mascot, Salacious Crumb

Jabba's majordomo, Bib Fortuna

Chewbacca and Boushh (Leia Organa)

Each cubicle hosts a *t'bac* hookah

Viewing grille to rancor pit below

Glowing stones beneath plaster walls hint at original B'omarr illuminated chapel

J'Quille, former lover of Jabba's rival, Lady Valarian

B'omarr pipe organ sealed behind false wall

Winch raises security door

Nar Shaddaa wind chimes

Stairway to entry portcullis

Back stairway

Taxidermied tauntaun head

To droid lift

Private backstage loft for band

Trap door to rancor pit

Power drum sports false skins

Jabba's prize trophy: Han Solo encased in carbonite

Jerba trophy head

Klatooinian drummer, Umpass-Stay

Trio of backing singers — Rystáll, Twi'lek Lyn Me, and Rodian Greeata

Jabba's private elevator

Double-headed Cane Adiss

Rappertunie tickles the Growdi water organ.

Elevator power supply

Trandoshan bounty hunter Bossk

Notorious bounty hunter Boba Fett

Chevin mercenary Ephant Mon owes his life to Jabba

Capo de tutti capo, Jabba Desilijic Tiure

Jerba meat roasting on a spit

C-3PO pressed into service as Jabba's translator

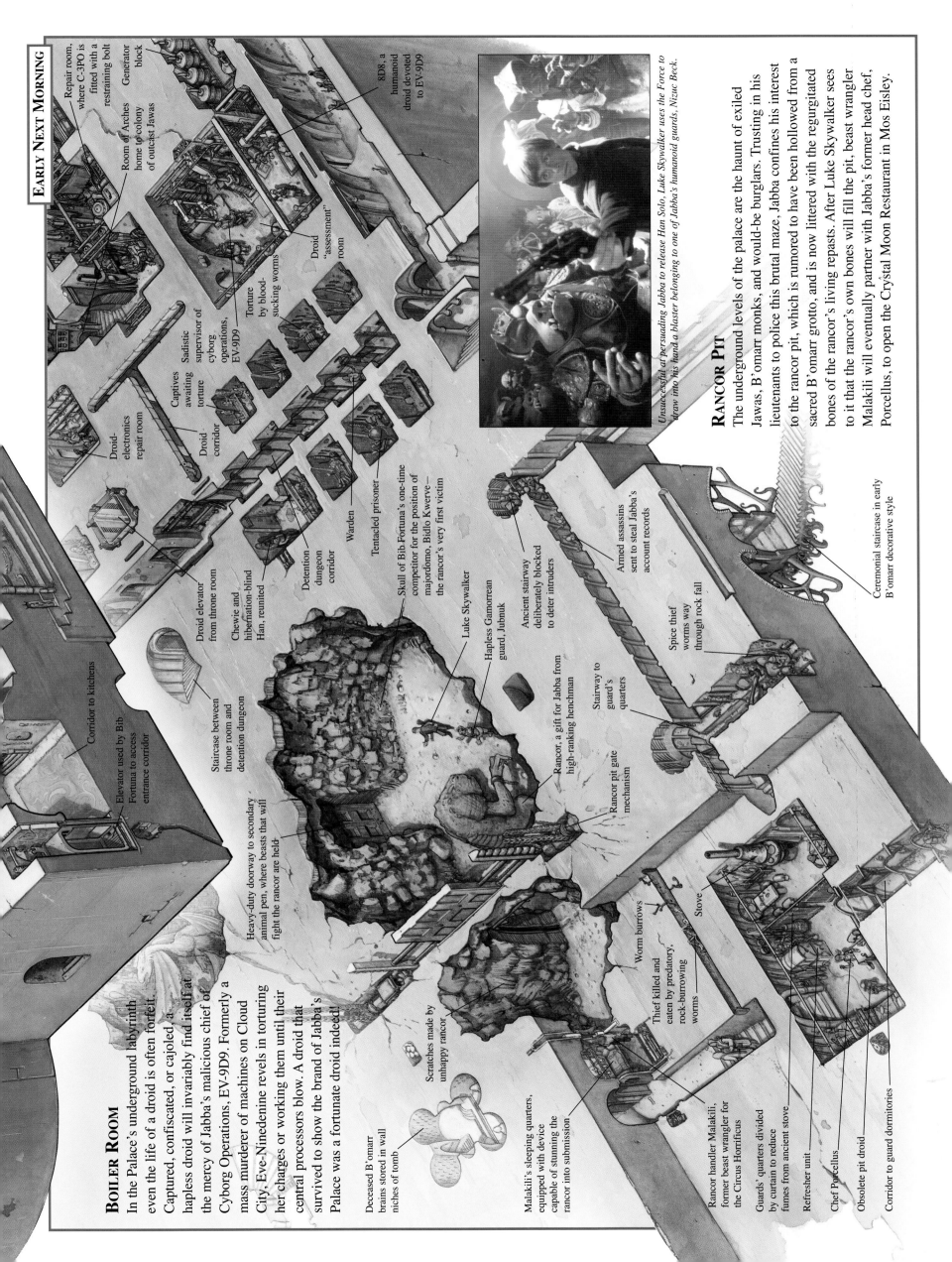

BOILER ROOM

In the Palace's underground labyrinth even the life of a droid is often forfeit. Captured, confiscated, or cajoled, a hapless droid will invariably find itself at the mercy of Jabba's malicious chief of Cyborg Operations, EV-9D9. Formerly a mass murderer of machines on Cloud City, Eve-Ninedenine revels in torturing her charges or working them until their central processors blow. A droid that survived to show the brand of Jabba's Palace was a fortunate droid indeed!

RANCOR PIT

The underground levels of the palace are the haunt of exiled Jawas, B'omarr monks, and would-be burglars. Trusting in his lieutenants to police this brutal maze, Jabba confines his interest to the rancor pit, which is rumored to have been hollowed from a sacred B'omarr grotto, and is now littered with the regurgitated bones of the rancor's living repasts. After Luke Skywalker sees to it that the rancor's own bones will fill the pit, beast wrangler Malakili will eventually partner with Jabba's former head chef, Porcellus, to open the Crystal Moon Restaurant in Mos Eisley.

Unsuccessful at persuading Jabba to release Han Solo, Luke Skywalker uses the Force to draw into his hand a blaster belonging to one of Jabba's humanoid guards. Nizuc Beck.

Repair room, where C-3PO is fitted with a restraining bolt

Generator block

Room of Arches home to colony of outcast Jawas

8D8, a humanoid droid devoted to EV-9D9

Sadistic supervisor of cyborg operations, EV-9D9

Droid "assessment" room

Captives awaiting torture

Torture by blood-sucking worms

Droid-electronics repair room

Droid corridor

Corridor to kitchens

Elevator used by Bib Fortuna to access entrance corridor

Droid elevator from throne room

Chewie and hibernation-blind Han, reunited

Warden

Tentacled prisoner

Skull of Bib Fortuna's one-time competitor for the position of majordomo, Bidlo Kwerve—the rancor's very first victim

Staircase between throne room and detention dungeon

Detention dungeon corridor

Luke Skywalker

Hapless Gamorrean guard, Jubnuk

Armed assassins sent to steal Jabba's account records

Ancient stairway deliberately blocked to deter intruders

Rancor, a gift for Jabba from high-ranking henchman

Stairway to guard's quarters

Spice thief worms way through rock fall

Ceremonial staircase in early B'omarr decorative style

Deceased B'omarr brains stored in wall niches of tomb

Scratches made by unhappy rancor

Heavy-duty doorway to secondary animal pen, where beasts that will fight the rancor are held

Rancor pit gate mechanism

Thief killed and eaten by predatory, rock-burrowing worms

Worm burrows

Stove

Malakili's sleeping quarters, equipped with device capable of stunning the rancor into submission

Rancor handler Malakili, former beast wrangler for the Circus Horrificus

Guards' quarters divided by curtain to reduce fumes from ancient stove

Refresher unit

Chef Porcellus

Obsolete pit droid

Corridor to guard dormitories

BATTLE OF ENDOR

WHILE IT COST THE REBEL ALLIANCE many lives, Bothan spies furnished the following intelligence: the Empire was constructing a second Death Star near the isolated Forest Moon of Endor. The Alliance had to strike before the facility was operational—but the Bothans also reported that the Death Star was protected by a massive defensive shield projected from a generator and dish network located on the surface of the forest moon. Thus, a desperate plan is hatched. Entrusting the *Millennium Falcon* to Lando Calrissian and Sullustan navigator Nien Nunb, Luke, Han, Leia, and a team of commandoes travel to Endor in a stolen Imperial shuttle, intent on destroying the shield installation.

1 Thanks to an old but serviceable Imperial code, the shuttle is allowed to land on the forest moon. The commandos set out for the shield-generator bunker, but are forced to engage a handful of Imperial scouts on speeder bikes. When two of the scouts flee, Luke and Leia take up the pursuit.

2 The 200-kph (124-mph) chase takes Luke and Leia on a zigzagging course through Endor's forest of mighty trees. Two more Imperials join the pursuit and Luke leaps onto the back of one of the bikes. He hurls the pilot into a tree, then drops back to deal with the second pair of scouts.

THE AFTERMATH OF VICTORY

The explosion of the second Death Star sent a rain of meteoric debris toward the forest moon, but the Rebel fleet was able to deploy shields and tractor beams to deflect debris away from their strike team on the surface. No sooner had the battle ended than Luke, Leia, Han, and Chewbacca, leading a small battle group of Alliance ships, were forced to respond to an emergency on the remote world of Bakura, where combined Alliance and Imperial forces thwarted an invasion by a galactic-edge reptilian species known as the Ssi-ruuk.

3 Thrown from her speeder bike, Leia regains consciousness to discover that she has company: a furry Endor native, whose crude spear is taller than he is. After sharing rations with the Ewok, and allying with him to dispatch two more Imperial scouts, Leia and Wicket head for Bright Tree Village.

4 Chewbacca inadvertently leads Luke, Han, R2-D2, and himself into an Ewok net trap. The astromech's circular saw arm cuts effortlessly through the net, only to drop the prisoners to the ground and directly into captivity, at the hands—and spears—of Teebo, Paploo, and other Ewoks.

5 Deprived of their weapons, Luke, Han, Chewbacca, and the two droids are marched to Bright Tree Village high above the forest floor. Much to Han's dismay, the Ewoks treat C-3PO with reverential respect, having taken him for a deity—even though the droid's programming prohibits impersonation.

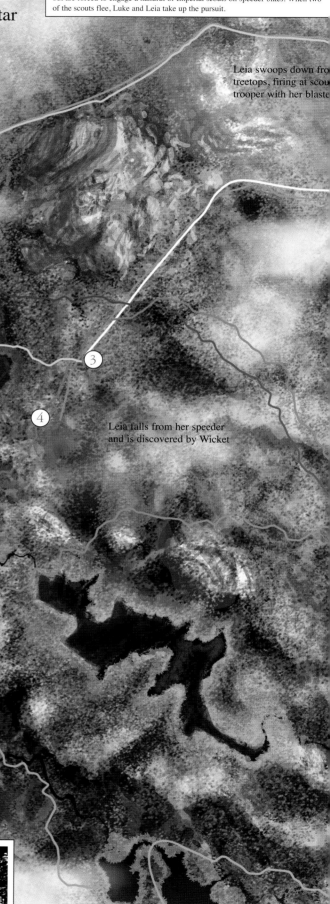

Leia swoops down from treetops, firing at scout trooper with her blaster

Luke leaps off his speeder bike and uses his lightsaber to slice control vanes of scout trooper's bike as it passes

Luke's speeder bike hits tree

Scout trooper hits tree

Scout trooper begins firing at Leia

Ewok trap

Scout trooper looks back to see explosion of Leia's speeder bike before crashing into tree

Bright Tree Village

Lake Sui home to Ewok stilt villages

Leia falls from her speeder and is discovered by Wicket

Ewok army and Rebels cross strait of Lake Marudi using Ewok-made rope bridge

N 0 1 km
0 1 mile

9 As the Ewoks deploy crude weapons against the Imperial troops—catapults, hang-gliders, and pouches of burning lizard oil—Han and Leia try frantically to reopen the blast door that has sealed the bunker. As Imperial AT-STs are being toppled by rocks and logs, Ewoks are felled by cruel blaster fire.

IMPERIAL INSTALLATION

Landing platforms serve as touch-down decks for shuttles and crafts of similar sizes, and as loading gantries for AT-ATs. The columnar legs of the modular platform house turbolifts, and the deck features a tractor beam emitter, multiple floodlights, and twin landing-zone target circles.

Corridors link loading gantries and turbolift shafts

Tractor-beam emitter

Turbolift

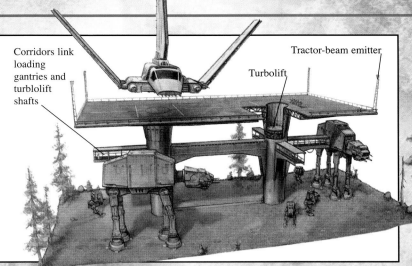

SPECIAL OPERATIONS

Several Rebels are decorated for helping to destroy the shield generator and thus render the second Death Star vulnerable to attack. Among these are Major Bren Derlin, who oversaw security at Echo Base and led the commando team at Endor, and General Crix Madine, who had defected from the Empire and was largely responsible for planning the raid on Endor's shield generator complex.

Leia pulls up into treetops

Scout trooper hits tree after blaster strike from Luke

Luke drops behind scout troopers, while Leia continues behind the lead trooper

Two additional scout troopers pull in behind Luke

Above-ground Imperial shield projector—underground power generator and shield projector complex spans an area 70 km (43 miles) in diameter.

Imperial turbolaser outpost at which Luke surrenders

Luke jumps over to scout trooper's bike and pushes trooper off

Luke and Leia on single speeder bike pull up alongside rear scout trooper bike

Extent of battle between Rebel/Ewok army and Imperial forces

Rear entrance to shield generator bunker

Imperial landing platform

Landing platform overlook

Scout trooper camp

Rebels land close to turbolaser tower outpost under guise of being parts and technical crew

Chewbacca shoots escaping scout trooper

ROUTE KEY

Leia, Luke, Han, Chewbacca, C-3PO, R2-D2, and troops of Rebel strike-team squad head toward shield generator bunker, via scout-trooper camp

Luke and Leia set off on single speeder bike

Scout trooper 1

Scout trooper 2

Luke hijacks scout trooper 2's speeder bike

Leia (solo) on speeder bike

Scout trooper 3

Scout trooper 4

Luke's route back to Han, Chewbacca, and the droids at scout trooper camp

Han, Luke, Chewbacca, and the droids search for Leia, are captured by Ewoks, and end up in the tree village

Rebel strike-team squad head to shield generator bunker

Wicket takes Leia to Ewok village

Luke's route to Imperial post, where he surrenders

Luke is carried to Imperial Landing Platform by AT-AT

Han, Leia, Chewbacca, droids, and army of Ewoks trek to rendezvous with squad at shield generator

6 With Han about to be roasted over a fire, Luke uses the Force to levitate C-3PO and his wooden throne over the heads of Ewok shaman, Logray, and Bright Tree Village chief, Chirpa. At C-3PO's command, Han, Luke, and R2-D2 are released from captivity and able to reunite with Leia.

7 Having sensed the presence of his son, Darth Vader arrives by shuttle at the landing platform for the massive shield generator installation, its perimeter safeguarded by Imperial war machines, including AT-AT walkers and AT-ST scouts.

8 Rebel commandos infiltrate the installation via the back door of the control bunker. Unaware that they have done just as the Emperor predicted, they are soon surrounded by Imperial troops. Outside the bunker, C-3PO acts as a momentary diversion, while the Ewoks prepare to launch a counter-offensive.

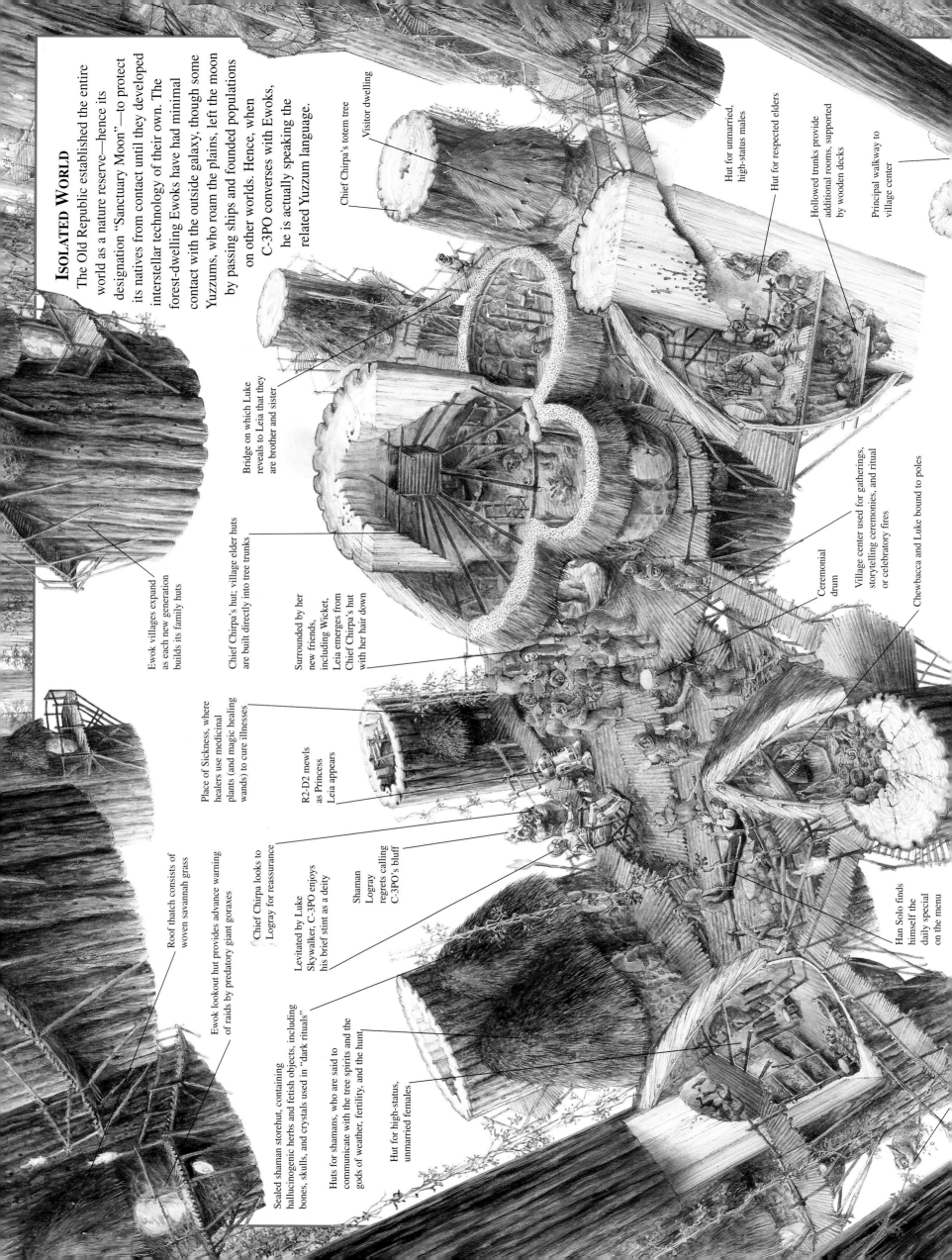

ISOLATED WORLD

The Old Republic established the entire world as a nature reserve—hence its designation "Sanctuary Moon"—to protect its natives from contact until they developed interstellar technology of their own. The forest-dwelling Ewoks have had minimal contact with the outside galaxy, though some Yuzzums, who roam the plains, left the moon by passing ships and founded populations on other worlds. Hence, when C-3PO converses with Ewoks, he is actually speaking the related Yuzzum language.

Visitor dwelling

Chief Chirpa's totem tree

Hut for unmarried, high-status males

Hut for respected elders

Hollowed trunks provide additional rooms, supported by wooden decks

Principal walkway to village center

Bridge on which Luke reveals to Leia that they are brother and sister

Ewok villages expand as each new generation builds its family huts

Chief Chirpa's hut; village elder huts are built directly into tree trunks

Surrounded by her new friends, including Wicket, Leia emerges from Chief Chirpa's hut with her hair down

Ceremonial drum

Village center used for gatherings, storytelling ceremonies, and ritual or celebratory fires

Chewbacca and Luke bound to poles

Roof thatch consists of woven savannah grass

Place of Sickness, where healers use medicinal plants (and magic healing wands) to cure illnesses

Ewok lookout hut provides advance warning of raids by predatory giant goraxes

Chief Chirpa looks to Logray for reassurance

R2-D2 mewls as Princess Leia appears

Han Solo finds himself the daily special on the menu

Sealed shaman storehut, containing hallucinogenic herbs and fetish objects, including bones, skulls, and crystals used in "dark rituals"

Levitated by Luke Skywalker, C-3PO enjoys his brief stint as a deity

Shaman Logray regrets calling C-3PO's bluff

Huts for shamans, who are said to communicate with the tree spirits and the gods of weather, fertility, and the hunt

Hut for high-status, unmarried females

MAGICAL FOREST

The bark of the conifer provide the Ewoks with an insect repellent, and the strong boughs supply material for bows, spears, slingshots, and catapult arms. In addition, the Ewoks share a mystic bond with the forests, with village shamans serving as intermediaries between the trees and the tribes. At the birth of each new tribal member, a life tree seedling is planted, and the guardian tree and Ewok mature together. On death, the Ewok's spirit takes up residence in his or her tree.

Rope swing provides shortcut to village center

Endor's ancient trees are surprisingly resilient against the heat of Ewok fires

The lively language of the Ewoks contains more than three dozen words for the conifers they refer to principally as "life trees"

Unmarried males can be called upon to help defend the village against predators from the forest floor

TREE HOME

Home to some 200 Ewoks, Bright Tree Village is situated approximately 15 meters (50 feet) above the forest floor. The trees in this part of the forest average only about 40 meters (130 feet) high, but the most ancient life trees elsewhere can exceed 1,000 meters (3,280 feet). Ewoks come down to ground level to forage for fruits and berries, and to hunt on wild ponies introduced to Endor by earlier human scouting parties. They also use smaller, native bordoks as beasts of burden.

At certain times of year, colorful orchids bloom in crevices of bark

The Ewoks love tall tales, music, and dance, and are quick to celebrate any occasion, such as the gentle capture of Luke, Han, Chewbacca, and R2-D2.

Condor dragons have been known to perch in high branches

Ewoks launch gliders from high in canopy

Food stored well above village huts

Ewok village constructed in under canopy

Sentries and unmarried males live below village

Forest floor covered with ferns, tree palms, and juicy mattberries

EWOK VILLAGE

THE SO-CALLED SANCTUARY MOON of the planet Endor is home to many millions of Ewoks, who live for the most part above the forest floor in tree villages. Clusters of crude thatch-roof huts hug the trunks of the enormous conifer trees, and are linked to each other and to the forest floor by ingenious walkways, rope bridges, and swings. The central part of the village consists of the chief's and village elders' huts, with an open platform where ceremonies and meetings take place. Families, including unmarried females, live in clusters of huts arranged outside the village center, with unmarried males living a little further away until they marry.

CONSTRUCTION PHASES

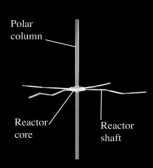

Polar column

Reactor core

Reactor shaft

1 The primary stage focused on assembling components necessary for construction of the main reactor core—approximately one-tenth the diameter of the entire structure—and the immense cylindrical polar column, which served to distribute power and stabilize the Death Star's rotational capabilities. A quartet of reactor shafts—bent 15 degrees in five places—extended outward to what would be the station's circumference, two of them emerging exactly at the equator. Capacitor panels were layered around the reactor core.

2 Subsidiary shafts were added to both the polar column and the four reactor shafts. (Some of these would later be used by Rebel starfighters to reach the surface of the station.) The equatorial, or "waistband," regions were constructed next, as they contained important docking facilities and the thrusters that rotated the station.

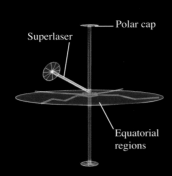

Polar cap

Superlaser

Equatorial regions

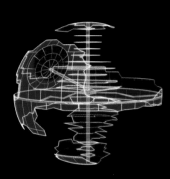

3 With the core and equatorial systems in place, construction crews next prioritized the building of the primary weapon. Only Vader and a few of the Emperor's advisors grasped that Palpatine's plan in leaving so much of the base unfinished was to deceive the Alliance into thinking that the superlaser would not be operational when the Rebels launched their attack.

4 As had been confirmed during development of the original Death Star, construction advanced most efficiently when the working surface allowed sufficient space for the greatest possible number of self-replicating construction droids. This was Moff Jerjerrod's justification for filling the station's interior in a piecemeal manner.

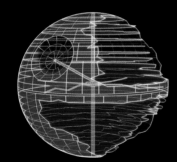

Command bridge located above lens, or dish, and patterned after bridge of original Death Star

Superlaser lens focuses nine tributary beams into primary beam of devastating, planet-destroying power

BASE OF OPERATIONS

Rising from the Death Star II's north pole, the Emperor's 100-story isolation tower was anchored to the station well before his arrival. This structure is surrounded by the greatest concentration of anti-starfighter gun emplacements, placed at intervals of as little as a few hundred meters, and all with improved fire control. Emperor Palpatine's Throne Room occupies one spoke of the penultimate story's quadripartite structure.

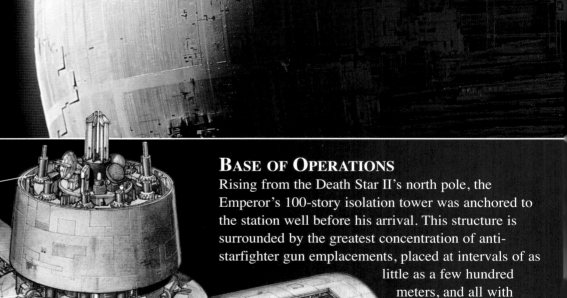

Docking ring for starships to moor at tower; smaller vessels, like Imperial shuttles, link via "umbilical" air tube

Sensors and communications arrays in summit

Imperial Guards stationed throughout the tower at all times

Laser cannons girdle crown

Circular viewports overlook weapons-studded city sprawls that surround the tower

Sleep chamber linked to medical diagnosis computers to monitor the Emperor's health

Receiving area, where Palpatine conspires and dictates his twisted thoughts on political power

Emperor's Throne Room

Other than to conduct routine maintenance, droids are not permitted in the upper tower

Holographic map of Galactic Empire indicates planets or star systems that are to be subjugated or punished

DEATH STAR II

SECRETLY CONSTRUCTED IN ORBIT around the remote Forest Moon of Endor, the second Death Star is over 900 kilometers (550 miles) in diameter—nearly a tenth the size of the moon itself. While the purpose of the original Death Star was to intimidate by a ruthless demonstration of power those planets and systems in league with the Rebel Alliance, the purpose of the second is, in part, to lure the Rebels to their doom at Endor. However, long before it is turned to space dust by the *Falcon*'s few well-placed proton torpedoes, it is the second Death Star that is doomed. For once, it is the Emperor who is wrong about a great many things, especially in his belief that Darth Vader would stand by while his son is being murdered.

In place of the two-meter (6.5-foot)-wide thermal exhaust port targeted by the Rebels at Yavin 4, the second Death Star possesses millions of millimeter (0.04 inch)-sized heat-dispersion tubes extending over the entire surface, each equipped with emergency baffle mechanisms to block excess-power surges

Areas immediately above and below equatorial trench are heavily armored

Equatorial trench contains nested hierarchy of lesser trenches, along with docking bays secured by atmospheric containment fields

Artificial gravity is localized throughout Death Star: in surface decks (the "city sprawl") gravity is directed toward core, allowing gun crews to stand "on" surface of the globe; in stacked inner decks, it is directed north to south

Surface "city sprawls" are linked to internal air circulation shafts and contain a high density of towers and surface weapons emplacements

Convoys of spaceships constantly supply construction crews with building materials

Construction droids work on future housings for hyperdrive motivator units

Active construction sites illuminated by sparks from countless welding droids; arc lights allow human crews to supervise operations

Construction droids work on future fuel-storage area

Arrays of temporary repulsorlift generators fill engineering sectors

Incomplete, the station reveals the axisymmetric planar structure of decks and shell-like structure of Quadanium outer skin

Quarters for shell-construction crews and energy replenishment stations for labor droids

DESTRUCTIVE MIGHT

The Death Star II is not parked in a naturally synchronous orbit above the Forest Moon, so remaining over one point on the moon's surface requires a considerable uplift force against Endor's gravity. Initially, the station was supported by a repulsorlift field projected from the same ground facility that would eventually supply the station with its defensive shield. Tales told by Ewok shamans relate that the extra weight on the moon's crust had dramatic side-effects, including massive groundquakes, land that shifted and buckled, and lakes that spilled out of their natural basins. After crushing the Rebel Alliance, the Emperor had planned to obliterate Endor as Moff Tarkin had Despayre (the construction site of the original Death Star) and Alderaan. In order to deliver a spectacular, planet-destroying burst, the station's hypermatter reactor would have to have been able to generate power equivalent to hundreds of super-giant stars.

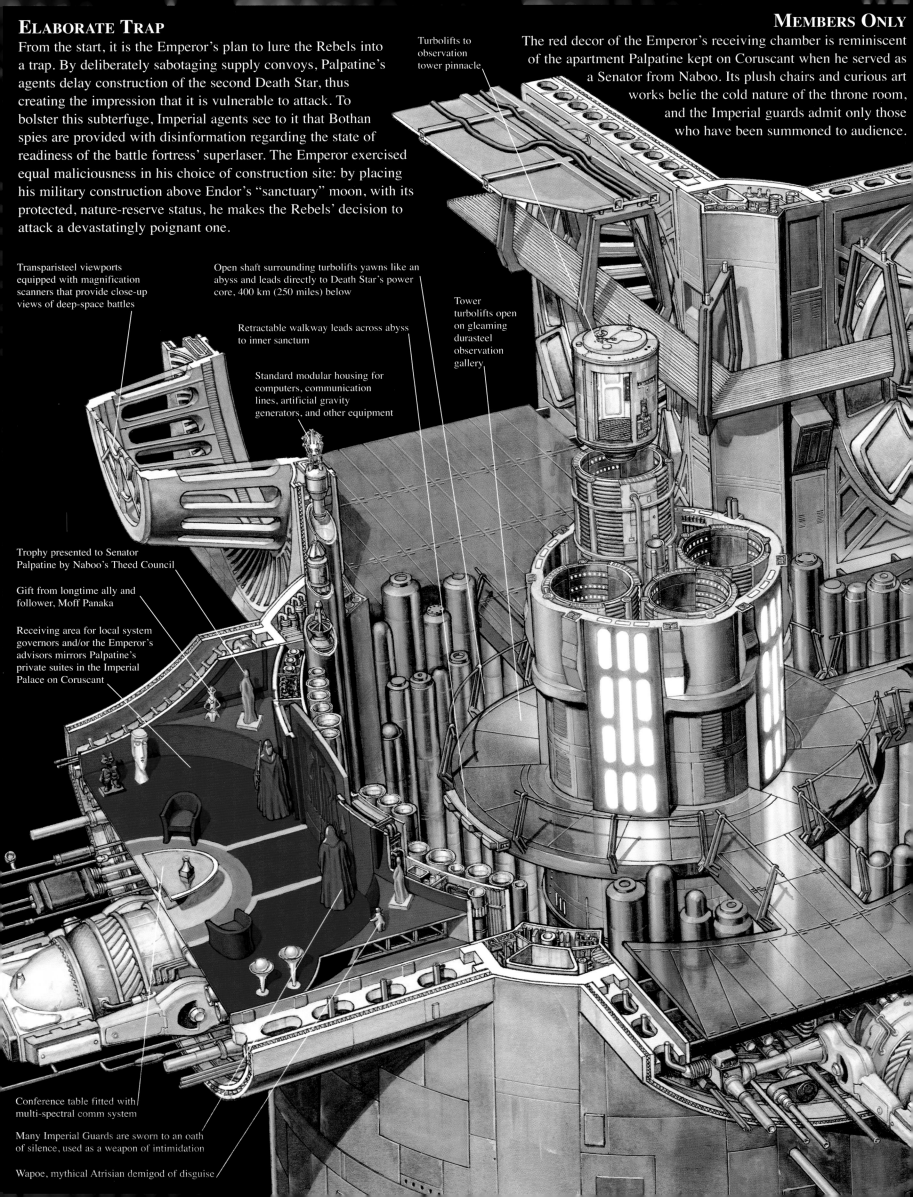

ELABORATE TRAP

From the start, it is the Emperor's plan to lure the Rebels into a trap. By deliberately sabotaging supply convoys, Palpatine's agents delay construction of the second Death Star, thus creating the impression that it is vulnerable to attack. To bolster this subterfuge, Imperial agents see to it that Bothan spies are provided with disinformation regarding the state of readiness of the battle fortress' superlaser. The Emperor exercised equal maliciousness in his choice of construction site: by placing his military construction above Endor's "sanctuary" moon, with its protected, nature-reserve status, he makes the Rebels' decision to attack a devastatingly poignant one.

The red decor of the Emperor's receiving chamber is reminiscent of the apartment Palpatine kept on Coruscant when he served as a Senator from Naboo. Its plush chairs and curious art works belie the cold nature of the throne room, and the Imperial guards admit only those who have been summoned to audience.

Turbolifts to observation tower pinnacle

Transparisteel viewports equipped with magnification scanners that provide close-up views of deep-space battles

Open shaft surrounding turbolifts yawns like an abyss and leads directly to Death Star's power core, 400 km (250 miles) below

Retractable walkway leads across abyss to inner sanctum

Tower turbolifts open on gleaming durasteel observation gallery

Standard modular housing for computers, communication lines, artificial gravity generators, and other equipment

Trophy presented to Senator Palpatine by Naboo's Theed Council

Gift from longtime ally and follower, Moff Panaka

Receiving area for local system governors and/or the Emperor's advisors mirrors Palpatine's private suites in the Imperial Palace on Coruscant

Conference table fitted with multi-spectral comm system

Many Imperial Guards are sworn to an oath of silence, used as a weapon of intimidation

Wapoe, mythical Atrisian demigod of disguise

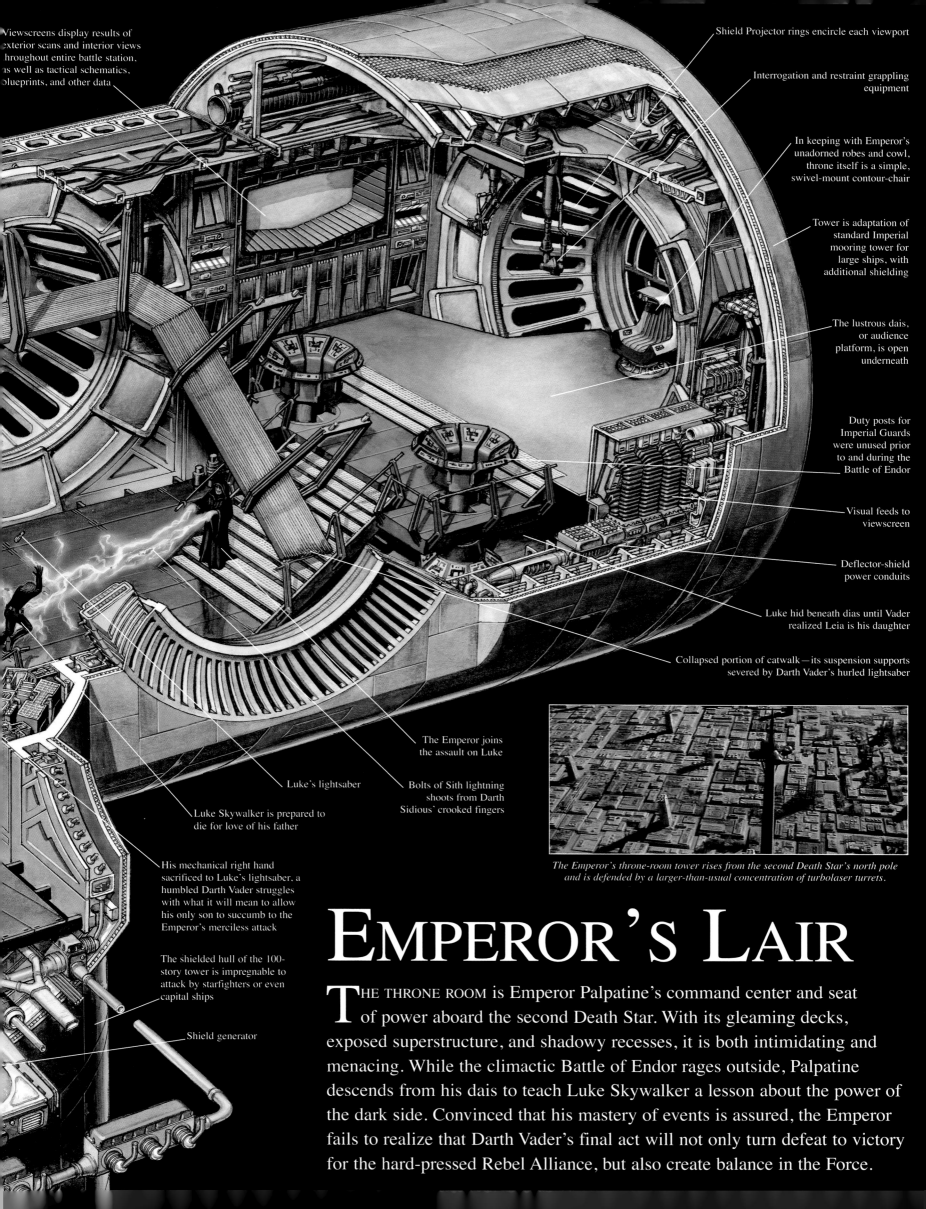

Viewscreens display results of exterior scans and interior views throughout entire battle station, as well as tactical schematics, blueprints, and other data

Shield Projector rings encircle each viewport

Interrogation and restraint grappling equipment

In keeping with Emperor's unadorned robes and cowl, throne itself is a simple, swivel-mount contour-chair

Tower is adaptation of standard Imperial mooring tower for large ships, with additional shielding

The lustrous dais, or audience platform, is open underneath

Duty posts for Imperial Guards were unused prior to and during the Battle of Endor

Visual feeds to viewscreen

Deflector-shield power conduits

Luke hid beneath dias until Vader realized Leia is his daughter

Collapsed portion of catwalk—its suspension supports severed by Darth Vader's hurled lightsaber

The Emperor joins the assault on Luke

Luke's lightsaber

Bolts of Sith lightning shoots from Darth Sidious' crooked fingers

Luke Skywalker is prepared to die for love of his father

His mechanical right hand sacrificed to Luke's lightsaber, a humbled Darth Vader struggles with what it will mean to allow his only son to succumb to the Emperor's merciless attack

The shielded hull of the 100-story tower is impregnable to attack by starfighters or even capital ships

Shield generator

The Emperor's throne-room tower rises from the second Death Star's north pole and is defended by a larger-than-usual concentration of turbolaser turrets.

EMPEROR'S LAIR

THE THRONE ROOM is Emperor Palpatine's command center and seat of power aboard the second Death Star. With its gleaming decks, exposed superstructure, and shadowy recesses, it is both intimidating and menacing. While the climactic Battle of Endor rages outside, Palpatine descends from his dais to teach Luke Skywalker a lesson about the power of the dark side. Convinced that his mastery of events is assured, the Emperor fails to realize that Darth Vader's final act will not only turn defeat to victory for the hard-pressed Rebel Alliance, but also create balance in the Force.

EXECUTOR COMMAND TOWER

RAISED ON A THICK STALK above the *Executor*'s dorsal technoscape, the 285-meter (935-feet)-wide command tower is practically a ship in its own right. It houses a profusion of vital components, including shield generators and communications sensors, as well as officers' quarters, briefing rooms, and escape pods for the vessel's upper-echelon commanders. Just above the center line of the forward face sits the command bridge. Faithful to Kuat Drive Yards' design philosophy of "terror styling," the tower is deliberately positioned in full view of any ship that might dare risk an attack.

Crewmen stationed at consoles below the Executor's *command-bridge walkway toil under the withering scrutiny of Lord Vader.*

Command tower

FATAL FLAW

With its gleaming command walkway and two-meter (seven-feet)-tall transparisteel viewports, the *Executor*'s bridge provides unobstructed views of quarries and kills. The ship's shielding—equivalent to the total power of a medium star—makes such displays of Imperial arrogance possible. Yet the vessel is not impregnable. At Endor, pounded mercilessly by the capital ships of the Rebel Alliance flotilla, the ship's shields fail. At that moment, the Rebels are able to strafe the command tower—and with the *Executor*'s navigation suite in ruins and defensive guns losing coordination, a careening A-wing destroys the bridge.

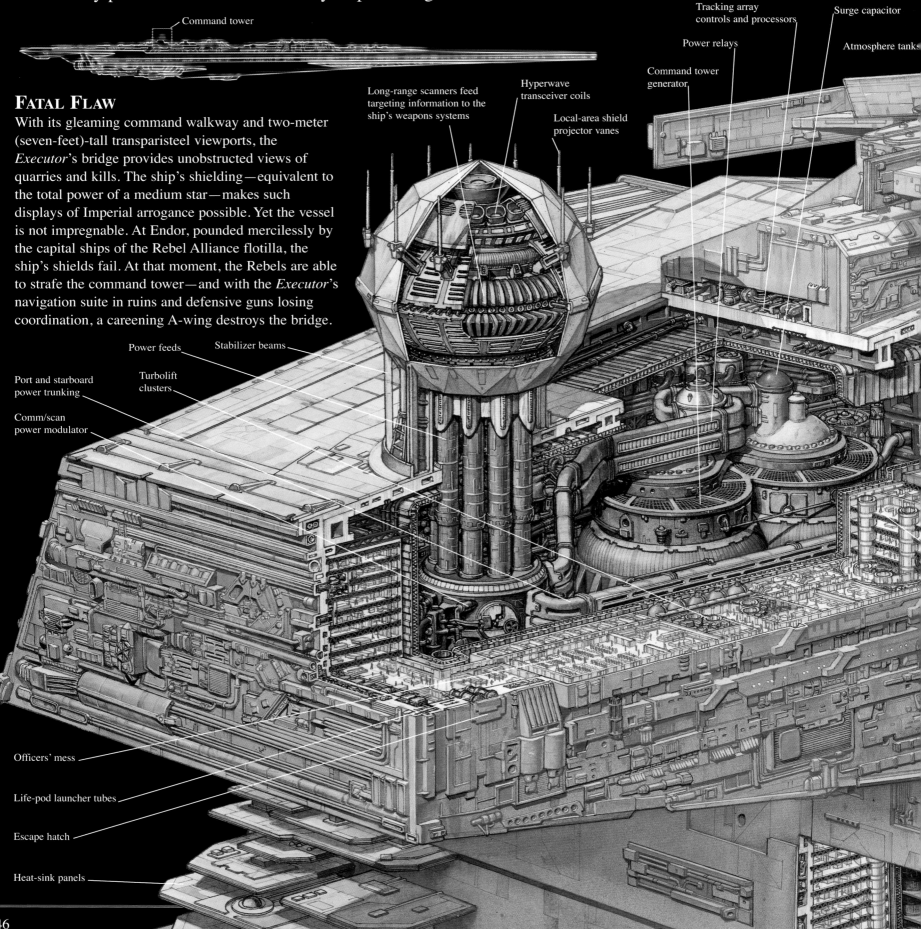

Tracking array controls and processors

Surge capacitor

Power relays

Atmosphere tanks

Command tower generator

Long-range scanners feed targeting information to the ship's weapons systems

Hyperwave transceiver coils

Local-area shield projector vanes

Power feeds

Stabilizer beams

Port and starboard power trunking

Turbolift clusters

Comm/scan power modulator

Officers' mess

Life-pod launcher tubes

Escape hatch

Heat-sink panels

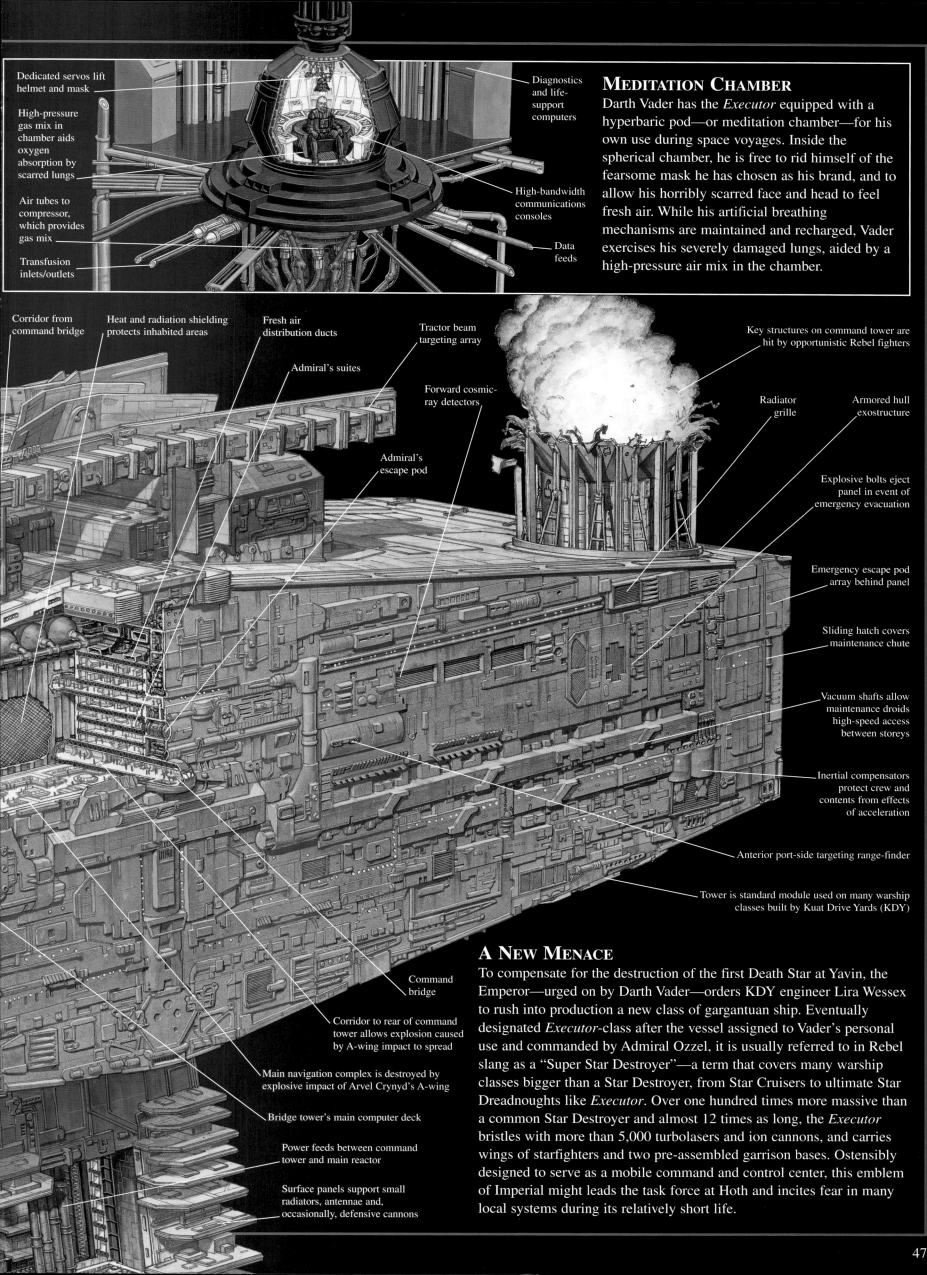

MEDITATION CHAMBER

Darth Vader has the *Executor* equipped with a hyperbaric pod—or meditation chamber—for his own use during space voyages. Inside the spherical chamber, he is free to rid himself of the fearsome mask he has chosen as his brand, and to allow his horribly scarred face and head to feel fresh air. While his artificial breathing mechanisms are maintained and recharged, Vader exercises his severely damaged lungs, aided by a high-pressure air mix in the chamber.

Dedicated servos lift helmet and mask

High-pressure gas mix in chamber aids oxygen absorption by scarred lungs

Air tubes to compressor, which provides gas mix

Transfusion inlets/outlets

Diagnostics and life-support computers

High-bandwidth communications consoles

Data feeds

Corridor from command bridge

Heat and radiation shielding protects inhabited areas

Fresh air distribution ducts

Tractor beam targeting array

Admiral's suites

Forward cosmic-ray detectors

Admiral's escape pod

Key structures on command tower are hit by opportunistic Rebel fighters

Radiator grille

Armored hull exostructure

Explosive bolts eject panel in event of emergency evacuation

Emergency escape pod array behind panel

Sliding hatch covers maintenance chute

Vacuum shafts allow maintenance droids high-speed access between storeys

Inertial compensators protect crew and contents from effects of acceleration

Anterior port-side targeting range-finder

Tower is standard module used on many warship classes built by Kuat Drive Yards (KDY)

Command bridge

Corridor to rear of command tower allows explosion caused by A-wing impact to spread

Main navigation complex is destroyed by explosive impact of Arvel Crynyd's A-wing

Bridge tower's main computer deck

Power feeds between command tower and main reactor

Surface panels support small radiators, antennae and, occasionally, defensive cannons

A NEW MENACE

To compensate for the destruction of the first Death Star at Yavin, the Emperor—urged on by Darth Vader—orders KDY engineer Lira Wessex to rush into production a new class of gargantuan ship. Eventually designated *Executor*-class after the vessel assigned to Vader's personal use and commanded by Admiral Ozzel, it is usually referred to in Rebel slang as a "Super Star Destroyer"—a term that covers many warship classes bigger than a Star Destroyer, from Star Cruisers to ultimate Star Dreadnoughts like *Executor*. Over one hundred times more massive than a common Star Destroyer and almost 12 times as long, the *Executor* bristles with more than 5,000 turbolasers and ion cannons, and carries wings of starfighters and two pre-assembled garrison bases. Ostensibly designed to serve as a mobile command and control center, this emblem of Imperial might leads the task force at Hoth and incites fear in many local systems during its relatively short life.

LONDON, NEW YORK, MELBOURNE,
MUNICH AND DELHI

DORLING KINDERSLEY

SENIOR ART EDITOR John Kelly
DESIGN ASSISTANT Jon Hall
ART DIRECTOR Mark Richards
DTP DESIGNER Dean Scholey

SENIOR EDITOR Simon Beecroft
CATEGORY PUBLISHER Alex Kirkham
PUBLISHING MANAGER Cynthia O'Neill Collins
PRODUCTION CONTROLLER Claire Pearson

LUCASFILM LTD.
ART EDITOR Iain R. Morris   EDITOR Jonathan W. Rinzler

First published in Great Britain in 2004 by Dorling Kindersley Limited,
80 Strand, London WC2R 0RL 2003
A Penguin Company

04 05 06 10 9 8 7 6 5 4 3 2

A CIP catalogue record for this book is available from the British Library.

ISBN 1-4053-0539-8

Colour reproduction by Media Development and Printing Ltd, UK
Printed and bound in Italy by L.E.G.O.

ACKNOWLEDGEMENTS

RICHARD CHASEMORE painted Tosche Station, Ben's house, the Cantina, the Death Star, Yoda's house, Jabba's palace, Jabba's throne room, T-16 skyhopper, Imperial landing platform and AT-AT landing barge. He would like to thank: Hilary for her support; Derrick Scrivener, Mike Godsell, Kevin Stokes, Steve Snooks, and Greg Smith for all their hard work building a fantastic studio.

HANS JENSSEN painted Lars' homestead, Echo Base, *Executor* command tower, Vader's meditation chamber, Cloud City processing vane, Cloud City, Emperor's lair, landspeeder, gas prospecting bike and carbonite block. He would like to thank: his partner Janine for her support and tolerance; Arne for his good advice; DK and Lucasfilm for their support; Richard Hartley for providing the best beer in the galaxy.

JOHN MULLANEY painted Mos Eisley and The Great Temple.

ROBERT E. BARNES created the maps of Tatooine, Battle of Hoth, Dagobah and Endor.

RICHARD BONSON painted the Ewok Village.

ALEX IVANOV took the photograph of Death Star II.

JON HALL created the schematics of Echo Base, the Death Star, and Death Star II construction sequence and the Dagobah planet image.

JAMES LUCENO would like to thank the following: Iain Morris, Jonathan Rinzler and Amy Gary at Lucasfilm for thinking of me for this project; Simon Beecroft, John Kelly and Alex Kirkham at DK Publishing for reminding me of just how inspired the Trilogy-era locations were, and what a fabulous city London continues to be. (Drinks at the American Bar, dinner at the Oxo Tower, David Blaine perched high above the streets... what could be more diverting?); my wife, Karen-Ann, for accompanying me on that trip; my sons, Carlos and Jake, for holding down the fort in Annapolis; brainstorming sessions with gifted artists Richard Chasemore, Hans Jenssen and John Mullaney were a collaborative delight, and listening to Curtis Saxton expound on subjects ranging from the physics of *Star Wars* to the sometimes dubious pleasures of living and working in Germany were nothing short of revelatory; Leland Chee and Sue Rostoni at Lucasfilm for ensuring continuity; and, finally, the authors of the many resource books I consulted during the course of this project, including Dan Wallace, Bill Smith, Shane Johnson, Stephen Sansweet, Kevin Anderson and Terryl Whitlatch.